Praise for *Lord Beaverbrook*

"Sheer poetry ... *Beaverbrook* reads just like one of Richards's novels about a country boy who grabs at fame and fortune only to find that the prize comes with infamy and misery."　　　　　　　　　　　　　　—*National Post*

"*Lord Beaverbrook*, by David Adams Richards, is a lovely book about a subject who is definitely difficult to love, or even to respect ... Masterful storytelling."
　　　　　　　　　　　　　—*Canada's History* magazine

"A biography that should rate four out of four on anyone's scale."　　　　　　　—*The SunTimes* (Owen Sound)

"Richards' portrait doesn't read like a dull, historical tome. It reads like a ripping good yarn."　　　　　—*Calgary Herald*

"An empathetic but unflinching biography."　　—*Maclean's*

Praise for the Extraordinary Canadians series

"These books are not definitive biography; rather, they are opportunities to deepen the relationship between Canadians of the past and Canadians of the present. May this dialogue continue, so that today's biographers themselves will be the subject of the next wave of writers." —*The Globe and Mail*

"The concise books are a vivid, 'character-driven patchwork' of modern Canadian history made relevant to modern readers. In other words, no dry academic tomes allowed … What's compelling about the Extraordinary Canadians series is that it draws you back to some of the original oeuvres—to Anne, to Carr's remarkable paintings or to Glenn Gould's Goldberg Variations." —*Vancouver Sun*

"Marvelous." —*Ottawa Citizen*

"Extraordinary Canadians features snappy, candid, highly personal sketches not meant to be definitive biographies. They are, instead, individual glimpses into the lives of some of the country's most prized achievers." —*London Free Press*

PENGUIN CANADA

LORD BEAVERBROOK

DAVID ADAMS RICHARDS is the author of the novels *Incidents in the Life of Markus Paul*; *The Lost Highway*; *The Friends of Meager Fortune*, winner of the Commonwealth Writers' Prize (Canada and Caribbean region); *River of the Brokenhearted*; and *Mercy Among the Children*, which won the Giller Prize and was nominated for the Governor General's Award and the Trillium Award. He is the author of the celebrated Miramichi trilogy: *Night Below Station Street*, winner of the Governor General's Award; *Evening Snow Will Bring Such Peace*, winner of the Canadian Authors' Association Award; and *For Those Who Hunt the Wounded Down*. His most recent non-fiction books are *God Is* and *Facing the Hunter*. His novel *The Bay of Love and Sorrows* has been made into a feature film.

SERIES EDITOR:
John Ralston Saul

Lord Beaverbrook

by DAVID ADAMS RICHARDS

With an Introduction by

John Ralston Saul

SERIES EDITOR

EXTRAORDINARY
CANADIANS

PENGUIN CANADA

Published by the Penguin Group

Penguin Group (Canada), 90 Eglinton Avenue East, Suite 700, Toronto, Ontario, Canada M4P 2Y3
(a division of Pearson Canada Inc.)

Penguin Group (USA) Inc., 375 Hudson Street, New York, New York 10014, U.S.A.
Penguin Books Ltd, 80 Strand, London WC2R 0RL, England
Penguin Ireland, 25 St Stephen's Green, Dublin 2, Ireland (a division of Penguin Books Ltd)
Penguin Group (Australia), 250 Camberwell Road, Camberwell, Victoria 3124, Australia
(a division of Pearson Australia Group Pty Ltd)
Penguin Books India Pvt Ltd, 11 Community Centre, Panchsheel Park, New Delhi – 110 017, India
Penguin Group (NZ), 67 Apollo Drive, Rosedale, Auckland 0632, New Zealand
(a division of Pearson New Zealand Ltd)
Penguin Books (South Africa) (Pty) Ltd, 24 Sturdee Avenue, Rosebank, Johannesburg 2196, South Africa

Penguin Books Ltd, Registered Offices: 80 Strand, London WC2R 0RL, England

First published in Penguin Canada hardcover by Penguin Group (Canada),
a division of Pearson Canada Inc., 2008

Published in this edition, 2011

1 2 3 4 5 6 7 8 9 10   (WEB)

Copyright © David Adams Richards, 2008
Introduction copyright © John Ralston Saul, 2008

Manufactured in Canada.

Library and Archives Canada Cataloguing in Publication

Richards, David Adams, 1950–
Lord Beaverbrook / by David Adams Richards ; with an introduction by John Ralston Saul.

(Extraordinary Canadians)
Includes bibliographical references.
ISBN 978-0-14-305595-2

1. Beaverbrook, Lord, 1879-1964. 2. Publishers and publishing—Great Britain—Biography.
3. Politicians—Great Britain—Biography. 4. Great Britain—Politics and government—20th century.
5. Newspaper publishing—Great Britain—History—20th century. 6. Philanthropists—
New Brunswick—Biography. 7. Businessmen—Canada— Biography. I. Title.
II. Series: Extraordinary Canadians

DA566.9.B37R52 2011   941.082092   C2011-902530-2

Visit the Penguin Group (Canada) website at **www.penguin.ca**

Special and corporate bulk purchase rates available; please see
www.penguin.ca/corporatesales or call 1-800-810-3104, ext. 2477 or 2474

For Jeffrey Carleton and Robert McCombs

CONTENTS

CONTENTS

by John Ralston Saul

How do civilizations imagine themselves? One way is for each of us to look at ourselves through our society's most remarkable figures. I'm not talking about hero worship or political iconography. That is a danger to be avoided at all costs. And yet people in every country do keep on going back to the most important people in their past.

This series of Extraordinary Canadians brings together rebels, reformers, martyrs, writers, painters, thinkers, political leaders. Why? What is it that makes them relevant to us so long after their deaths?

For one thing, their contributions are there before us, like the building blocks of our society. More important than that are their convictions and drive, their sense of what is right and wrong, their willingness to risk all, whether it be their lives, their reputations, or simply being wrong in public. Their ideas, their triumphs and failures, all of these somehow constitute a mirror of our society. We look at these people, all dead, and discover what we have been, but also what we can be. A mirror is an instrument for measuring ourselves. What we see can be both a warning and an encouragement.

These eighteen biographies of twenty key Canadians are centred on the meaning of each of their lives. Each of them is very different, but these are not randomly chosen great figures. Together they produce a grand sweep of the creation of modern Canada, from our first steps as a democracy in 1848 to our questioning of modernity late in the twentieth century.

All of them except one were highly visible on the cutting edge of their day while still in their twenties, thirties, and forties. They were young, driven, curious. An astonishing level of fresh energy surrounded them and still does. We in the twenty-first century talk endlessly of youth, but power today is often controlled by people who fear the sort of risks and innovations embraced by everyone in this series. A number of them were dead—hanged, infected on a battlefield, broken by their exertions—well before middle age. Others hung on into old age, often profoundly dissatisfied with themselves.

Each one of these people has changed you. In some cases you know this already. In others you will discover how through these portraits. They changed the way the world hears music, thinks of war, communicates. They changed how each of us sees what surrounds us, how minorities are treated, how we think of immigrants, how we look after each other, how we imagine ourselves through what are now our stories.

You will notice that many of them were people of the word. Not just the writers. Why? Because civilizations are built around many themes, but they require a shared public language. So Laurier, Bethune, Douglas, Riel, LaFontaine, McClung, Trudeau, Lévesque, Big Bear, even Carr and Gould, were masters of the power of language. Beaverbrook was one of the most powerful newspaper publishers of his day. Countries need action and laws and courage. But civilization is not a collection of prime ministers. Words, words, words—it is around these that civilizations create and imagine themselves.

The authors I have chosen for each subject are not the obvious experts. They are imaginative, questioning minds from among our leading writers and activists. They have, each one of them, a powerful connection to their subject. And in their own lives, each is engaged in building what Canada is now becoming.

That is why a documentary is being filmed around each subject. Images are yet another way to get at each subject and to understand their effect on us.

There has not been a biographical project as ambitious as this in a hundred years, not since the Makers of Canada series. And yet every generation understands the past differently, and so sees in the mirror of these remarkable figures somewhat different lessons.

What strikes me again and again is just how dramatically ethical decisions figured in their lives. They form the backbone of history and memory. Some of these people, Big Bear, for example, or Dumont, or even Lucy Maud Montgomery, thought of themselves as failures by the end of their lives. But the ethical cord that was strung taut through their work has now carried them on to a new meaning and even greater strength, long after their deaths.

Each of these stories is a revelation of the tough choices unusual people must make to find their way. And each of us as readers will find in the desperation of the Chinese revolution, the search for truth in fiction, the political and military dramas, different meanings that strike a personal chord. At first it is that personal emotive link to such figures which draws us in. Then we find they are a key that opens the whole society of their time to us. Then we realize that in that 150-year period many of them knew each other, were friends, opposed each other. Finally, when all these stories are put together, you will see that a whole new debate has been created around Canadian civilization and the shape of our continuous experiment.

David Adams Richards is absolutely right. No Canadian has ever been as powerful on the world scene as Max

Aitken, Lord Beaverbrook. If there was any possibility that a colonial could push an empire around and change its intent, this was it. And God knows Beaverbrook tried. If he saw himself as a failure in the end it can only be because empires can't be shaped by colonials or outsiders of any sort. To believe they can is part of the delusion of the special relationship. Empires have neither friends nor allies. And they don't have special relationships. They have power and self-interest. The trick is to exploit them without getting in their way. Beaverbrook is the example for all time of just how far a colonial can go. But as he would tell you, it just isn't far enough.

I was not yet fourteen years old when Max Aitken died. I make it clear that what is written here about the actual events in his life are documented in other places—by his biographer A.J.P. Taylor, or his friend Peter Howard in his book *Max the Unknown;* by his biographer Gregory P. Marchildon in his book *Profits and Politics;* by the biographers of Churchill, like Manchester and Jenkins, or Stalin, like Alan Bullock, or by the imp Max himself in his book *My Early Life*. However, this book's interpretation of these events, both his successes and failures, and why they happened the way they did, is my own.

CHAPTER ONE

Beaverbrook

In so, so many ways, Max Aitken's success came from his failure to do what he wanted to do.

He was born in Ontario and moved with his family to Newcastle, New Brunswick, when he was one year old. He started his own paper when he was eleven, tried law and political campaigning at seventeen, sold bonds when he was twenty, became a millionaire at twenty-five, went to England, was knighted at thirty, and became a Lord of the Realm at thirty-eight. He was instrumental in helping one of the great politicians of the era, Liberal David Lloyd George (a man who would betray him soon after), become prime minister of Britain in 1916. He did the same for his friend and fellow New Brunswicker Conservative Bonar Law in 1922, had a decades-long feud with Conservative British prime minister Stanley Baldwin, and was a lifelong friend of Sir Winston Churchill. (At times the only friend Churchill had.) He was courted by and counselled kings and statesmen, bedded scores of women, was influential in helping artists create modern Canadian art, and was the greatest newspaperman in the world by the age of forty. He was by far the most influential and important Canadian of the twentieth century and, arguably, could be credited with almost single-handedly saving Western civilization.

Yet he was reviled in his adopted country of England, looked upon as a colonial, and hated by the aristocracy as an upstart. He was snubbed by those he most wanted to impress, and betrayed by those he trusted and helped. The heroic and historic role he played on the world stage from 1910 to 1945 is almost forgotten in Canada (like so much else about our history). And of all the things he hoped for, the one he most wanted, the thing for which he, as a financial genius, would have given up everything else—an Empire Free Trade agreement between Britain and her Commonwealth of Nations (much like the Free Trade agreement in place now between Canada and the United States)—never came to be.

The people he knew in Canada and Europe were the Who's Who of the political, financial, and artistic world for three generations. Even if their voices are now receding into history, make no mistake about this. When I mention David Lloyd George or Stanley Baldwin or Bonar Law or First Sea Lord Fisher, I am naming some of the most influential men in a Britain that still maintained its Empire. This was a British Empire still at its height (if we consider its height from Waterloo to the Somme), and in a way it was Max Aitken's as much as anyone's.

There were three great moments in his life, intersected by others almost as momentous.

The first was the Canada Cement fiasco of 1910, which made him a multimillionaire.

The second was the part he played, as a sitting member of the Conservative Party in the British House of Commons, in the ascendancy of Machiavellian Liberal radical David Lloyd George to the position of prime minister in a war-weary England of 1916.

The third was his being called to cabinet by Winston Churchill as minister of aircraft production, and then as minister of war production and supply from 1940 to 1942.

Among these significant events were many others: buying and selling Rolls-Royce and being knighted in 1910; being elected to the British parliament in 1912; buying the *Daily Express* in 1916; being granted a lordship in 1917; becoming minister of propaganda (or minister of information) in the First World War coalition cabinet of David Lloyd George; bedding various glamorous women; and failing in his Empire Free Trade campaign, on which all his hopes rested.

CHAPTER TWO

Early Times

He had a face that, even into late middle age, suggested an exuberant imp, an arrogant scallywag. In a way he never escaped his habit of insolence and a feeling of being able to slingshot over others to get what he wanted. Nor did he ever escape his fascination with his own ability, and a tendency to dogged self-promotion. At times it didn't even matter who his audience was—as long as he had one. He was a vaudevillian, always on stage.

In his memoir, *My Early Life*, he mentions Sir Winston Churchill watching him writing one day, and asking him what he was doing:

"Writing," Beaverbrook said.

"Writing—about what?"

"Me."

"A good subject," Churchill responded. "I have been writing about me for fifty years, and with excellent results."

The son of a Presbyterian minister, William Aitken, Max Aitken was born in Maple, Ontario, in May 1879, and arrived at the newly built manse in Newcastle, New Brunswick, with his family in 1880. This was the Newcastle he loved and romanticized in stories he told to people like Winston Churchill and Soviet dictator Joseph Stalin. It was in Newcastle that all his formative learning took place. This was where he started out as a newspaper owner at the age of eleven, and, at seventeen, ran the first political campaign of R.B. Bennett, future prime minister of Canada. Beaverbrook—the name he would later take for himself—was first the name of the stream he, and most everyone else from the town (including me), fished in as a child.

He donated much to this town of Newcastle, and to its twin town of Chatham. There was the town hall. There was the Sinclair Rink, where I played hockey, named in honour of a Mr. Sinclair who first loaned him money to travel to a university he never cared for. There was the Beaverbrook Rink in Chatham, and the Old Manse Library, established in his former home. It boasted signed first editions of books by H.G. Wells and Rudyard Kipling—men he knew, but whose books he never read (too wordy for him)—which I found in the second-floor reading rooms when I was a boy. (His own room, a little alcove of a place up on the third floor, had been turned into the French section of the library. That was where I first found Montaigne and Villon—and where I hid during school hours. Just as Max ran from the house into the street to escape the harshness of his lessons, so I often ran from the school to his room to do exactly the same thing.)

When he was born, Edison was introducing the light bulb, and Hitler was not yet a glimmer in a Bavarian's eye. Hitler would be born in 1889. Winston Churchill had been born five years before Aitken, in 1874, at Blenheim Palace. Joseph Stalin, destined to become the supreme dictator of the Soviet Union, was born six months after Beaverbrook, in December 1879. I mention these three men in conjunction with Beaverbrook, not because he played as great a part in twentieth-century history as they did, but because he played an indelible part in their achieving—or not achieving—certain of their aims. Of course he was closest to Sir Winston Churchill, a fact pointed to by anyone who admires Beaverbrook for his political savvy and his ability to survive the storm-tossed politics of the age. (Of course, one must admire Churchill for this to be the case, and I admire Churchill a good deal.)

When it comes to growing up far from the centre of the world, and overcoming this obstacle to become instrumental in it, he had most in common with Comrade Stalin of the Soviet Union. Beaverbrook came from the same kind of backwater stock as Stalin, which would alienate him from many of those in the polished circles he would attain. (He would always be set apart, first as a Maritimer and then as a Canadian.) Both were disliked for their accents as much as their demeanour. Both were small, both were tough, both were despised by their own children, both were feared—though here, Joseph Stalin, as one of the greatest malevolent presences of the twentieth century, takes the lead.

Of course, Churchill and Beaverbrook, flaws aside, helped to hold the world together in 1940, when Hitler and Stalin had traded ambassadors. There is a moment here when a reader might say Beaverbrook does not belong in this company; there is a moment when, as financier of the Spitfire aircraft and ferry campaign for bombers, one may not only think but be grateful that he does. For a while Beaverbrook held the same position in Britain as Albert Speer did for Hitler after 1943 (without the slave labour) or that Malenkov, Voroshilov, Kaganovich and others did for Stalin during the same period (without all the terrible internecine spilling of blood).

BECAUSE HIS FATHER was distant and austere (one Aitken sibling remembers that the word *love* was never mentioned in the house), Max Aitken would look for a father figure most of his life. In fact this was one of his main quests: to prove himself worthy to an ideal father. And in some ways it was his undoing.

His small bedroom on the third floor of the Old Manse Library (which is now the Beaverbrook Museum) looks down the hill toward Pleasant Street, to the town's financial district, where shipbuilders and bank owners lived. Night after night, long after his parents thought him asleep, he must have stared out that small window toward the great town below, wondering about all the lively events taking place. He must have heard the trains in the distance, coming and going from Montreal to Halifax and back. Like most boys, he must have longed to be outside when he was in.

Newcastle (now the City of Miramichi) was—and, in some ways still is—a great town with a grand tradition, and a mixture of Empire Loyalists, Irish, Scots, and French. There were very rich men here, and also a streak of poverty born of class and lack of education. Houses that guarded the finer streets; and others without heat in winter.

How many men and women in Newcastle would Max have known? Judging by his later gift for making acquaintances, I would bet that, by the age of nine, he knew them all—from grand lumber barons who attended his father's church to my own poor Irish relatives who lived in Injun Town five blocks away!

As the son of the minister, he served as pallbearer at the funerals of young boys and girls, and was given white gloves to carry the casket. This task filled him with nightmares, until he decided to burn his gloves after each internment. This dispensed with his fear, and showed a resilient and inventive temperament at an early age.

He would leave the house early, and stay outside as much as he could. Every day he walked along Pleasant Street, or through the town square (where a bust of him now sits, and his ashes are interred). He would stop to chat with older men—having his picture taken with a few of them one winter afternoon near Howard Williston's Jewellery shop, an old wooden building that was still there when I was young. In the picture he stands on the far right side, gazing out at us all, smiling, a boy of seven.

He would spend his days far away from the manse. Then he would walk home along the King George Highway at night, knowing he was in trouble with his parents, and try to sneak in the door. I can picture him there in the small foyer, in direct view of anyone sitting in the front room.

He said of himself that he was a "cat who travelled alone," but often he must have been a lonely kitten. From the age of twelve on, he seems to have been so much on his own that it makes me sad when I think of it—and, except for one picture of him on the steps of Harkins Academy, all the pictures taken of him are with adults. (Only when he is an old man are there pictures of him with children.) He never seems to have mentioned a real childhood friend. Perhaps he looked upon children as children—and perhaps he never saw himself as one of them. By the time he was twelve, the games they played were not his games.

AITKEN ALWAYS BELIEVED he was a master of his fate. In fact he wrote about it in his book *My Early Life*, and specifically mentioned it often enough to his friends.

Yet it is strange for Max to say this, when at the same time he claimed that an accident with a mowing machine when he was a child caused the brilliance that propelled him to such heights.

If we believe him, and I have no reason not to, he was an ordinary boy, until one day, as he was running alongside a hay mower that was being pulled by a team of quarter-horses, he got his sleeve caught in its mechanism (probably the small thresher that ran perpendicularly just behind the horses) and fell beneath it, hitting his head on one of the studded iron wheels. He was taken to bed, and, when he awoke, he claims he was a very different boy in one respect: he could think and understand things much more clearly. After this accident, he had an uncanny ability to comprehend why and how money was made and used. It was as if, from the time he was twelve, he was always three or four moves ahead of everyone else.

I believe there is only one of two ways to think of this event with the mowing machine. Either the accident was simply that, an accident, or Divine Providence caused it. Though Max Aitken said he never trusted to luck or chance, the idea of predestination is a Presbyterian article of faith, and Max used to argue for this as a young man, especially with R.B. Bennett. How much faith he had in predestination has always been open to speculation. Nor in the end are we privy to his private beliefs. (Late in life he still remembered the inspirational songs sung at church, and he mentioned Calvin as one of his heroes.)

But there can be no other way to think of this enormous event in his life—either accident, and the world is random, or Providence, and it was a miracle decided by forces over which he himself had no control, for a purpose of which he had at best limited understanding (as Tolstoy mentions about the entire human condition at the very end of *War and Peace*).

If God or Providence had suddenly decided to make him brilliant, he still had to use that brilliance. As we will see, he did not always morally succeed in this. But still and all, his life is a miraculous and continuous catalogue of events which, not destroying him, made him stronger.

I suppose he would have become a target of even greater scorn in some circles if he had dared say it was Divine Providence! (We must never forget how small the sense of Divinity is among our educated middle classes.)

There might be one sign however. As a child he picked potato bugs from gardens and gathered wood for a Mr. Manny to earn a few cents. Yet, after that injury, Max became a newspaper boy, a correspondent, and an efficient calculator and transactor of money matters. He also became even more of a rogue. But is that surprising? The son of the manse, he must have found the stricture unbearable, the hours for study and worship tedious and restricting. The manse was a wonderful old house to visit, but to live there with a stern father who demanded decorum and a pedestrian outlook was another thing entirely.

Hardly a boy in the land would be happy inside a manse when there were rough boys outside, especially with a father who was said to have had "a voice like God almighty" and who spared him little love. In some ways he must have felt he would never be able to please Reverend Aitken. And so he spent more and more time outside with older men he knew he could entertain. This pattern started very early and became one of the main pursuits of his life: acting the scallywag, the juggler of tales, entertaining others by embellishing his own story.

In his teenaged years, he sought out rogues and adventurers. I am sure his fascination with life itself, and his zeal to understand it in all its mystery, propelled him. Here he lingered at a bakery, there at an office, down at the wharf talking with sailors from the square riggers and the schooners that came to transport timber overseas. Listening to the stories of woodsmen, of veterans from the Crimean War, of sailors who had been to Europe, who had walked the streets of London itself, he stored up information and a longing to be part of it.

There is not much talk of sports and young Max Aitken—except for fishing. A friend of mine has a picture of Max's older brother Traven (who died of an accidentally inflicted gunshot wound) playing football, but there are none of Max.

He must have spent many a night alone in that bedroom on the third floor, realizing that, in some way, whatever he did, he would never please his father enough. And so he would have to go. Do I think he was lonely? Yes. Do I think he felt unloved? Absolutely. But then I know how outsiders are continually forced to the outside by people who pretend to be concerned on their behalf. At Harkins, my schooling was very much like his, though he was a millionaire by twenty-four and I didn't make ten thousand dollars until I was thirty-five. Still, we had more than a little in common, and it went beyond being born and raised a block and a half from one another.

HIS ARGUMENTS at the house were probably fierce, and most likely continual. His big head would be seen peeking around the doors of his siblings' rooms continuing confrontations, and his sisters and brothers were more than a little tired of him. There were six brothers and sisters, several with unusual names that their mother thought romantic, like Rahno (a sister) and his brother Traven. There was also Magnus, Arthur (who later became an American) and Allan (a lawyer in Newcastle). Not to forget Maxwell, of course.

But from all reports, even his own, Max was the one who caused the disruptions. When he was twelve, his father said he should learn to translate the Latin phrase *Gallia est omnis divisa in partes tres*, about Gaul being divided into three parts. Max answered with the quip that he would much rather learn how to divide twenty-five cents into three parts. I know we can cringe at that—but not completely. There is an old Islamic saying that the dreams God gives you must be pursued in order not to offend him. Perhaps this is all Max was doing—in fact it is all any of us do. And he was brave enough to tell his father what his dream was: to become in a way his father's worst nightmare, a man who looked to the things of the earth to satisfy earthly desires.

There is a story—possibly apocryphal, as so much about Max Aitken is—about the time when, as a boy, he sold eggs from his own hens. Once, when he had an order for more eggs than he could supply, he went to his mother's kitchen and borrowed the rest. The next afternoon the woman who ordered these eggs asked him what kind of hens he had, for half the eggs were already hard-boiled.

"I knew the thunderstorm we had yesterday would affect my hens," he replied.

That sounds straight out of *Tom Sawyer*, but Sawyer's and Aitken's habits weren't so different, and were in some ways entirely alike. One could very easily imagine Aitken convincing others to paint the fence for him on a warm summer day. And that was the problem, even for those who loved him. He was an imp and a scallywag, but his motives always came back to self-interest. Once the ultimate winner, he could then turn about and be generous. But he wasn't prepared to lose. I am sure that, for the rest of his life, some part of him was trying to divide the twenty-five cents into three. That he was in large part success-ful benefited many who found it distasteful to hear him say it.

"I never thought he would be a success at anything," the headmaster of Harkins said. This shows the one ingredient most principals and headmasters need: blindness to any real talent. And what is worse, they are proud to admit this tendency.

Max must have come up against this early—must have in some ways been terribly frustrated by it, and in other perverse ways loved it. It was at Harkins where he learned that everyone had to be a mark. He told his fellow students he could count the hairs on a teacher's moustache, and made money promoting this idea. (He couldn't count the hairs, but he knew well enough they couldn't either.) Asked to write something about himself, he carved his initials into his desk. The desk was there when I was a boy, and has since been misplaced. I wish I had been the one smart enough to take it. I am sure Max would have.

They called him "Moccasin Mouth," because of how large a mouth it was. And one boy told him that if God had made his mouth any larger he would have had to remove his ears. That is a great line, and one that I am sure Max would have loved to use himself—if the mouth had been on someone else.

He was drawn to public life, and began to publish a paper in his own house and deliver it on the street by himself. It was filled with interesting things about the town, about local politics and industry that he had managed to observe. I'm sure he made up some very likeable lies in order to please. That was also one of his early characteristics: embellishment. Perhaps he was trying to see what he could get away with. To my mind, only two kinds of youngsters do this: one is trying to take on the world, the other is trying to please his headmaster.

But his father did not see the worth of this paper, especially when Max wanted to print it upstairs at the manse—on a Sunday. So Max turned his attention to corresponding, not telling the newspaper—the *Telegraph*, in Saint John—how old he was.

When it was reported to his father, erroneously, that Max the correspondent was writing sarcastic tributes about various people and events in town that would damage their reputations, his father reprimanded him severely with threats of hellfire. (I am sure this was a more than constant threat.) Max decided to run away to Kent County, where his father came to retrieve him, saying all was forgiven. In truth Max had not been the author of such libel, so there was nothing to forgive. (Or at least it hasn't been proven. I am almost sure

Max would have delighted in writing yarns about anyone in town if he could get a laugh and get away with it. He understood how to get under people's skins, and loved to do it all his life.)

Still, at fourteen, Max had noticed the world and the world was beginning to notice him. He was going to be a part of it one way or the other. He was seething with the enthusiasm of youth to do something beyond the restrictions of his parents' house, and to do it well. He resumed his correspondent position for a dollar a column. But this was only one of the many ways he had of making money. The idea of making money was paramount with him from the time he was a boy, so there must have been lots of talk about money at the house. He must have listened to his mother and father talking about scrimping and saving, going without, and priding themselves on this ability. Though the family was not poor, it was not rich either.

He knew he could do better. This is something else that I believe shaped his personality and his course in the world: the idea that the manse was God-driven, and the outside world—down Pleasant Street and beyond—wasn't. Once out those doors and down the steps of that manse, he was free to be less than God-driven, because he saw how others were less than God-driven and he could match them, but his dad could not. He could outsmart and out-scallywag, and out-think any of them. He could and did and would discombobulate them—for his father's sake. (Well, of course for his own sake, too.) Did it bother his conscience? Yes, all his life! Years later, in England, he bought a racing stable. Realizing how his father would have disapproved of such things, he renamed it Calvin House. (And too, there might have been some mischievousness in doing so.)

About 1894, he was given a position at Lee Street's pharmacy on the Town Square in Newcastle, also for one dollar a week. An incident here shows his almost pathological bent for trouble.

He tended to completely ignore the doctor's prescriptions and make up his own, trying out different remedies as he went, like a mad little concocter. One day he was caught doing this and the dollar a week was forfeited to his talent for mischief. He was sent home to his parents, and one can imagine the rumours about town.

(It is amazing that this was the standard by which people were paid—that is, not the currency but the amount. It seems to me that all of Max's early endeavours resulted in the tribute of one dollar per week. Never in my readings about him did he complain about this amount, so it must have been fair and standard wage. His father, however, did. Parsimony was perhaps a necessary habit for a minister, but it was awful how he showed it. Once when young Max was living in Halifax, Rev. Aitken sent him a box of books. Reluctant to spend one dollar on the shipping cost, he sent it at the much more reasonable—and slower—rate of thirty-eight cents. He instructed Max to pay the thirty-eight cents.

IT IS LUCKY he did not die, for it's likely there were many that wanted to kill him. I'm sure most couldn't see him succeeding at anything. Max, however, could. He was sure of his genius and probably painfully aware that others did not have it—and, worse, did not recognize it in him. Perhaps they thought he would some day be a schoolteacher, a labourer, or a clerk. These were all activities that would have made him moderately successful in their eyes. Then he wouldn't have been such a threat.

But Max was destined for other things. His boyhood was a fermenting ground for rudimentary ideas of business and money-making. And the area was not so primitive as one might think. The Miramichi, among other things, was the birthplace of the Cunard Shipping Line (which was later sold to England's White Star Line, which built the *Titanic*) and of some of the greatest lumber barons in the country. Its industries were the physical industries of lumber and the sea.

These were extremely sophisticated industries for the time, and Max would have delighted in scampering about the town, discovering the promise in such things. This and playing pranks were his two main pastimes. For the rest of his life he couldn't seem to do without either. His boyhood was a time for driving his parents and siblings to distraction. (His older sister Rahno once threw him down a flight of stairs in an attempt to kill him.) Perhaps nowadays the boy would have been put on medication. And what would have happened to his empire then?

One cannot help but think of him as an elderly man at dinner with potentates from the Empire—ladies and lords, members of parliament—watching them with a mischievous glint in his eye, as his friend Peter Howard says, like a cat ready to pounce. The idea, if he ever had it, that once he was finished with school he wouldn't have to deal with mundane people ever again, proved to be wishful thinking. He would have to deal all his life with those who thought inside the box, who had dutifully done their lessons, who could get high marks in everything except thinking for themselves. Often he would have to fight them alone. In fact, in the end, they were the ones who did him in. Like a cat being pecked to death by ducks.

CHAPTER THREE

Lawyer's Apprentice and Campaign Manager

There were many law offices on the Miramichi, in which many boys of Max's age and demeanour articled. This certainly was one way into the greater world, and young Aitken knew this. By the age of fifteen he was ready to leave his father and mother and try life on his own. I believe the only champion he had at that time was himself.

He knew one of the finest law firms was that of Tweedie's, across the river in Chatham. So he waited his chance, and took advantage when it came, and one spring day about 1896 he met Mr. Tweedie, portly and proud of it, and a locally famous lawyer, on the ferry boat travelling from Newcastle to Chatham. Engaging him in conversation, the ever-optimistic Max appealed for a job as law clerk. It was the same kind of chance meeting he would have a few years later with John Stairs of the Union Bank of Halifax.

He had so many of these chance meetings in his life, one wonders how random they were, and how many times he took the ferry ride before this particular chance meeting occurred. So Moccasin Mouth, and double-dealer, went as law clerk, smiling all the while.

LATER HE SAID he went into law at Tweedie's because R.B. Bennett was a lawyer there, and Max wanted to emulate Bennett, who was already a local politician. That is the same R.B. Bennett who would one day become leader of the Conservative Party and prime minister of Canada. Max's childhood longing to be accepted by older men, and his precocious ability to keep them entertained, would become over time instrumental in the affairs of great men and of nations. Was his father ever jealous of this, or did he have too much else to think about? For, even by nineteenth-century standards, Max was young when he went out on his own.

R.B. Bennett, twenty-six at the time, and a former teacher in Douglastown, a village between the two main Miramichi towns of Chatham and Newcastle, was a high-strung, driven political animal, who could quote Disraeli and had legislative ambitions. (Anyone who could quote Disraeli would be welcome in my house, at least once.) He was the first, and therefore the most important, father figure of the many Max Aiken would seek out.

At seventeen, Max ran Bennett's very first political campaign, for alderman of the newly chartered town of Chatham, New Brunswick. This was in 1896. Bennett was a church-going Methodist and a teetotaller, and Max says this is where they parted company (intellectually speaking), which gives us the first indication that the Beaver was imbibing when he was sixteen or seventeen. On the Miramichi at that time, of course, this might have been a relatively mature age to begin. He talks about a back room at Adams's (my mother's name but no relation) where he boarded, and the lumberman William Richards (my grandfather's name but no relation), and about parties and card games and drinking that went on. I am sure they did, and I am pretty sure Max would have a hand in some of it. He was far too exuberant not to. He was too gregarious not to have a devil-may-care attitude. The nights were too wondrous not to join in, the girls—for which he always had a weakness—too pretty. But I also know something about the drinking excesses of youth, and Max seems to be the kind who was too energetically ambitious to have spent too much of this energy drunk. Miramichi drinking habits are dangerous, and peer pressure is deadly. Many young men (and women) succumb to this temptation. I believe his determination to succeed in the world, to make father figures proud of him, prevented wholesale inebriation, or at least curbed it. Also, among the fashionably drunk, it is never popular to be your own man. Max was always his own man.

He has a story about what he was like at that time, which shows the kind of man he was to become. Wanting to go out to a dance—he was already an habitual skirt-chaser, something which would plague him, and others, most of his life—he asked his landlady, Mrs. Adams, to sew up a small hole in his best pair of pants. She told him she would do it for fifty cents. He did not have fifty cents, but, going into the living room, he saw fifty cents sitting on the fireplace mantel. He took it to Mrs. Adams, saying, "Here's your fifty cents." He did not lie. He got the job done. Was this calculated or spur-of-the-moment devilment? The second seems likely, but the fact he told the story shows how important quick thinking was to him. It would serve him well many times in the future. It would serve the world well, too—but it would also lessen him in the eyes of men, and cause much pain.

HE GOT ON at Tweedie's law firm as a clerk, and did run Bennett's first foray into local politics. But Tweedie was to say later that Max was into so many different ventures, he sometimes wondered if Aitken was working for him or he for Aitken. He also mentioned that people would come to the door seeking out Max Aitken's various talents rather than to inquire about a legal matter. Of course this was said in hindsight, and might not have been said at all if Aitken had not become Lord Beaverbrook.

In some ways, R.B. Bennett, as father figure, was the greatest influence in Beaverbrook's life. Max never forgot him, and never forsook him, even in the 1930s when Canada blamed Bennett, then prime minister, for the woes of the Depression. (This was reflected in the name Canadians gave the cars that, because of the price of gas, had to be hauled by horses: "Bennett Buggies.")

But loyalty was one of Max Aitken's admirable traits. It was a trait he always let you know he had, and a trait that would work against him at crucial moments in his life.

Another trait, exuberant but inadvisable, was the tendency to give out promises on Bennett's behalf during the campaign. He would ride around the streets of Chatham on those quiet evenings on Bennett's bicycle, handing out leaflets—and promising everything from new docks to new sidewalks to new jobs, if only Bennett were elected. So it was here that the notion that Max Aitken was a notorious liar got its official start. It's an accusation that is true in part, yet often his promises were more mischievous than manipulative, given out with a brazen, what-the-hell attitude. There is a difference between mischief and calculation, and I believe one should also have the grace to realize he was seventeen.

Though the child is father of the man. "Here's your fifty cents" was in fact an omen of things to come—and some of them would grow darker as the years went by.

On election night, with the results in, Bennett the victor thanked his young charge profusely for such a successful campaign. The morning after, when he learned what he supposedly had promised to men he didn't know, and to some he never liked, Bennett was furious.

"You will never handle a campaign of mine again," declared Bennett, who always had his eyes on the greater prize.

"Well, I'll never again give wholesale promises of that sort," Max concurred.

Both statements, of course, were false.

THERE WERE MANY things for him to do—go to dances, and run campaigns, and be a man-about-town at seventeen— estranged from his father and the awful stricture of church. Out in the world you had to be a very different man than in the manse. It was the difference between being a gunslinger and a sodbuster. His life seemed to prove that he had made an early choice between them.

Having parties was better than sitting listening to a sermon. He had listened to enough of those. Playing cards was better than reading verse. Ice-boating on the river in the winter with some sweet maiden was better than studying about Gaul (he doesn't mention one particular girl in his life at this time, so perhaps there was more than one, or perhaps, because of his looks, he was rebuffed. He had, after all, a mouth like a moccasin).

Still, life seemed idyllic for a time. His dreams at this point were probably very locally focused, for he was a clerk in the firm of his hero, Bennett. I am sure he could no more see London, England, from his office window than he could see Sheldrake Island, which was at one time a leper colony for his and my countrymen.

However, late in 1897, our future prime minister, R.B. Bennett, seeking better opportunity in the West, left for Calgary. Max Aitken suddenly discovered the offices of Tweedie to be cold, cramped, and unceremoniously boring, as A.J.P. Taylor states. His dream of always being Bennett's right-hand man, and helping this man to great success, was gone. What would he do? He needed someone to pin his sleeve to. Or did he? Maybe he could be what

Bennett was. So he simply advertised the fact that he had taken over Bennett's position in Tweedie's firm.

He told his family prematurely that he was to take Bennett's chair, something for which, he believed, as office clerk and lawyer apprentice, he was in line.

"Yes," I can hear him telling his startled Mom and Dad, "I will have my name on Tweedie's door. I will become the barrister for the church—when it needs me!"

He desperately wanted them to be proud of him. He wanted the world to know him. He had talent, enormous talent, that they didn't register, and it was like an unformed substance in him. He would brag about it until they understood it was there. In some ways he would do this all his life.

It was a humiliation, then, to learn that the chair would be given to a man named Mitchell, the son of a Father of Confederation from Newcastle, who had done his law training at university. It felt like a betrayal by Tweedie himself. (The firm did, as a courtesy, later on put his name on the door—as Lord Beaverbrook.)

However, his assertiveness had rankled—and in some ways frightened—Tweedie, who could not get a handle on the boy, or control his exuberance.

(This is how R.B. Bennett secretly felt about Aitken, too. There was too much of the showman, the circus act, the juggler on one leg, and his need to prove himself was too exhausting for these older men. He would never be made welcome in pleasant society; to have him near was almost always an embarrassment. It was an embarrassment they, like many others, were later to hide from him, whenever they needed his exuberance and showmanship. To tell the truth, I am not sure he ever caught on.)

So the boy was let go.

But Aitken's life is often an example of how bitter disappointment, supposed failure, and disaster can at times help you immensely. If he was master of his own fate, this then was a twist he had not expected, one which in the past sent him at first under the mechanics of a mower, and now to Saint John, and then to the great world beyond.

CHAPTER FOUR

The Great World Beyond

The idea that the world is your oyster comes from the fact that you haven't found where in the world your oyster is. To have succeeded in Chatham might have put a stop to Max's future—whereas not having succeeded in Chatham, or Saint John, meant that, having ambition, he had to push farther afield. But in addition to ambition, he must have had some sense that what he wanted to do still eluded him. If he had had his name etched upon Tweedie's door as Max Aitken, lawyer, I can almost guarantee it would never have appeared there as Lord Beaverbrook some years later.

In retrospect, it is fortunate too that the eighteen-year-old who went to the Saint John law school, wide-eyed at all the shops and offices about King's Square, was rejected there as well.

This is a poignant incident, though Max always made light of it. He believed that, as one of the brightest young students (though he rarely if ever actually went to class), he would be invited to the law school dance (an invitation-only affair). He rented a tux, using safety pins for cufflinks. That day he waited and waited for the invitation that did not come. Finally, he walked past the building where the dance was being held to hear the music and see the dancers, to look at the pretty girls. It seemed to him that his world had crashed again, and again he had failed miserably. He stood in the dark listening to the orchestra and wondering why God had cast him in the role of a failure. There were certainly moments in his life over which he had no control. It must have been a lonely moment on that dark street. He put his hands in his pants pockets and walked away.

Very despondent, as he was to be many times in his life, he decided on the spur of the moment to head West, to meet up with his "friend" and father figure, Bennett, who at that time in 1898 was in another campaign for office. It is probable, as A.J.P. Taylor says, that Bennett didn't want this young fellow near him, and had no inclination to help him. Besides, Max had made unsavoury friendships and had bought into a bowling alley. But Max, the grand enthusiast, ended up doing what Bennett once swore he would never do again: he ran Bennett's campaign in Calgary. He went into the poorer section of the town with whisky and promises. Very likely because of this, Bennett won as a member of the Legislative Assembly for the North West Territory—but once again Max had promised too much. Bennett, realizing Max would only be, as he said, "a drummer," or salesman, slammed the door on him, and told him to go.

Max then headed north to Edmonton for one reason only: to meet James Dunn, another older New Brunswicker, and a successful financier, who would move to England in 1905 and be knighted in 1922. He was known for saying the "west must pay tribute to the east." In a way, Dunn was startled at the brashness of this young fellow, who was now selling insurance and given to wild and exhaustive self-promotion. He still seemed something like that circus act, a con man. Dunn, wanting rid of him too, told Max to go back home, to be out of his hair. Max first tried another venture, transporting meat to the miners and prospectors in the North, but the meat went bad, and he was left with a debt he couldn't pay.

Max returned to Saint John. Perhaps he was lonely for the Maritimes, for the company of his siblings, with whom he always remained in touch. (In fact, he was to send each of them money over the years, and provide for his father as well.) One must remember he was eighteen or nineteen years of age, selling insurance and now being a sometime correspondent for the *Montreal Gazette*.

Back in Saint John, he sold some insurance to a clothing store owner, and bought a suit costing eight dollars—which he couldn't pay for all at once, and attempted to pay off in instalments of fifty cents at a time. (In fact, he didn't pay off the suit until years later, when he remembered the debt.)

So, here was young Max, trying to succeed in a world with men twice his age. An imitator, they were to say in later years, of older men. Another way to put it: you can't be Billy the Kid without a bounty on your head. In some ways Max was just this sort of gunslinger, and would have a price on his head from here on out. And a lot of Pat Garretts, posing as friends, as well.

Many nights he must have spent alone on the streets of cities, hungry and almost broke, wondering what he was going to do to make a name for himself. Often he must have been hungry for real companionship as well. Many nights he must have thought, as a lonely, rather unattractive youngster: "What will become of me?"

HE TELLS US he went fishing in Nova Scotia with three acquaintances when he was about to turn twenty-one. Up until now, he believed he was a loafer. How strange it is to look back at a boy of twenty, who had already run two political campaigns for a future prime minister, had sold insurance, had written for the *Montreal Gazette*, had studied law, and had travelled the country, calling himself a loafer. But he says this is how he felt, and I have no reason to believe otherwise.

At any rate, he tells us, it was on his trip to Nova Scotia that a person, whose name Max was later to forget, spoke to him around a campfire of duty and honour and dedication, and pronounced the world a better place for those who had these qualities. Max states in his memoir, *My Early Life*, that it was then he decided to change his life.

But did he change his life much at all? He said he became ambitious. But he always was. In fact, he seemed to be the most ambitious youngster ever to walk Newcastle's King George Highway. He was a hustler; in some ways he always would be. But one should not necessarily count that as a complete failing.

The story about the fishing trip has something of a morality tale about it—one that Max himself may have believed in more and more as the years passed. He was always an embellisher of small events, making them into big ones as time went by, especially if they contained moral lessons from his youth.

"MAY YOU LIVE in interesting times" the Chinese curse goes. Max did. A new century was coming.

Sandford Fleming's railway crossed the country, the last spike hammered, and a boom was on. New inventions were the bread of progress, and Max was aware of them all. There were electric lights, and telephones, and train travel, and the first motor cars were seen as strange mechanisms in the towns he visited. There was also the bond market, where you invested some money in companies and took some of the profit back at the end of the fiscal year.

Max became enthralled by this form of enterprise, and began to sell bonds door to door along the rural coasts of New Brunswick and Nova Scotia. To him, it seemed tantamount to making money for nothing. He would take the train to a certain station and walk into the country, a young, five-foot-five-inch, irascible bundle of promises. On those country roads of 1899 and 1900, with the houses a mile apart or more, the days must have been long and tedious, at some points arduous, and seemingly hopeless, the weather unpredictable. Still, Max was persuasive enough to coax money from people who would not otherwise give it, and he had a penchant for selling. That is, he could sell bonds to people who hadn't had the slightest idea of what a bond was before he knocked on the doors of their forlorn houses.

As time went on, he paid out his dividends faithfully and honestly, and made some money doing it. He was therefore a hustler still, even though he did not hustle in pool halls or at card games (and one wonders how much of this he ever did, and how much of what he reported would be put down today to youthful embellishment).

How many young men in the province were aware of bonds in the year 1900? Less than 1 percent, probably. In fact, how many businessmen knew about them? Well, Max, just coming into manhood, did. That is, he was a businessman. In his life everything, including newspapers, was for profit. He would, like Lord Thomson of Fleet and Lord Black of Crossharbour (two other Canadian newspaper barons who, like Beaverbrook before them, made their controversial ways to the top of the newspaper world), look at the world of newspapers as an industry—one in which you had a duty to secure public opinion on your side, but a business nonetheless, like all his other enterprises. But in 1900, newspapers were in his future.

He dined at small restaurants with ordinary folk, had grand ideas, and lived in rooming houses with other small businessmen. His life at this time was taken up not only with making money but with making the lifeblood of money: the right contacts. Slowly he met the right people. Some of them even showed an interest in this brash young wheeler-dealer from the Miramichi. This was the life outside the manse. He tells us that when he was a boy he had romantic visions of the world, drawn from the tales of King Arthur. Perhaps in some strange way he saw himself as a prince conquering the world. If he did, he was about to conquer more of it than most. Alexander the Great, when told that greatness would befall anyone who could unravel the Gordian knot, simply took his sword and cut it. Max Aitken, like Alexander the Great, had one weapon with which to cut through the same sort of Gordian knot—his brash self-confidence.

CHAPTER FIVE

Mr. Stairs of the Union Bank of Halifax

One day, while on a train to Halifax, Max sat down beside the owner of the Union Bank of Halifax, Mr. John Fitzwilliam Stairs, and tried to sell him a typewriter. There are other stories about how the two met, but I like this one best. Max, sitting there with a typewriter, that new-fangled gadget that would speed the process of writing tenfold. (Did he think it would make him a better writer? Of course he did; there was a crassness in his enthusiasm for newness.) Still, this must have been fascinating and ingenious, and anything new that was ingenious was glorious to him.

It is not reported if Mr. Stairs bought the typewriter. Probably not. But he was a very astute businessman who recognized Max Aitken as being the real deal. Max sold himself on that train to Stairs, sold his ability and his abundant self-confidence.

There is, however, another version of the story, in which Max, not being hired by Stairs, simply went to the Halifax office, sat down at a desk, and began to work. Stairs, at first angered, realized the potential of someone so daring and hired him. Either story—or a half-dozen others—will do.

The Stairs family controlled many profitable businesses, such as Scotia Steel, financial companies such as Eastern Trust, and Maritime industrial companies as well. They also sold securities in utility companies in the West Indies. All of this was endlessly intriguing to Max, who was for the first time introduced to the real workaday world of corporate enterprise, seeing how political and business antagonists worked, squabbled, and then, for the sake of money, put squabbles aside.

Max got on with Stairs, but not with others in the company hierarchy, who looked on him as an upstart and brash outsider. But this new world fit Max like a glove; he was aggressive and sure of himself and learned that he knew and could operate within the world of business. Max Aitken was more than willing to take chances the older generation would not.

"Stealing a bank"—as Max described it himself in *My Early Life*—was the work Stairs put him to. That is, John Stairs wanted to consolidate his family's Union Bank of

Halifax with a smaller bank in Windsor, Nova Scotia, and sent Max to find out if he could buy it out. Did he see the unscrupulous side of Max, and was he ready to use it? We do not know. Certainly he must have recognized Max's talent for convincing people to do things they had not thought of doing before. And, lucky for Aitken, he lived in an age when we actually had enough moxie in Canada to allow private citizens a range of enterprise they have no recourse to now. It would be very difficult to be a Max Aitken now in New Brunswick. At any rate, it was not the case then that the restrictions on our own people precluded great enterprise.

But even in those days, not one in ten thousand would have been able to accomplish what Max Aitken did. Within three weeks, the bank in question was under Stairs's direction, and Max took a ten-thousand-dollar bonus from the sale (or, at least, so he tells us). This was to be his first merger.

Over time, he would become one of the great merger manipulators in the world, wheeling and dealing with the most famous men of his time, using as his playing field both Britain and Canada. And it all started with trying to sell a typewriter.

NOW HE WAS on his way. At a time when most people earned perhaps eight hundred dollars a year, Max walked away, he states, with that ten-thousand-dollar fee. It was good money and, what was better, he had Stairs's gratitude and trust. As ever, he enjoyed the gratitude, the trust, of older men, and needed their endorsements. Stairs did like him, and did help him to see the world from the top down. He would never have to look from the bottom up again.

"By hiring Max as his personal secretary, Stairs gave Aitken a personal and first-class introduction into the world of Canadian high finance," writes Gregory P. Marchildon in his book *Profits and Politics*, the most extensive and best book on Beaverbrook's financial genius.

So Stairs helped fund Max's next venture: a finance and bond company. Stairs received a percentage of the profits, and Max, at least as he claimed, did all the work. He was now under the Stairs umbrella, the Scotia Group, which had vast holdings in banks, coal mining, farming, and utilities. Max began to look at doing business beyond Halifax, tending toward the West Indies. He had decided he was not ready for what he called "the Montreal or Toronto Sharks."

Later, a biographer from Toronto would exclaim at how terrible it was for Max to say this, being as he was such a shrewd, wily, and underhanded shark himself. What was terrible? Was it that he said this, or that he was more of a shark than they? If he had failed, would their laughter at this country bumpkin have compensated him for his loss? What it does show, however, is to what degree he was considered an outsider.

He began investing in railroad and utility companies in Cuba and Trinidad and Puerto Rico. If a certain utility company he had his eye on wouldn't allow his investment, Max would start a rumour that he was going to set up a rival company, which usually frightened the owners. His method was no more unscrupulous than a McDonald's setting up beside a Burger King, or an Irving by an Esso. He was also not above offering bribes, in a country of bribe-takers.

Though he felt he was doing a man's work, as Marchildon states, he was looked upon as John Stairs's private secretary by other family members, even though John Stairs, up until his untimely death, included him in every major negotiation and, over the next few years, he would become very influential in directing the Scotia Group in its endeavours. By his proficiency, he would earn the trust of one Edward Clouston, president of the Bank of Montreal.

For a time, Max was headquartered in the grand Halifax Hotel—and for much of the rest of his life he would have private lodgings in hotels, where he conducted business and entertained. Hotels also seemed to be right for Aitken. From the days when he used to slip out from under the gaze of his parents and walk the streets of Newcastle, Max Aitken really had no home. Hotels were one way to show this, to intimate to others that he was a traveller. A traveller and a loner. That is why he ended up so far away.

Soon everyone had heard of him, and, as he was introduced about, by himself or by others, he met General Charles Drury, who had taken charge of the Halifax Garrison from the British—a very notable thing. One other notable thing about General Drury was his daughter Gladys.

CHAPTER SIX

Marriage in the New World

From all accounts, Max married a wonderful woman in Gladys Drury. She brought with her an aura of charm and elegance, and her family brought connections in a higher society. The love between them was mutual—at least to the extent that Max could manage. (Of course he would be unfaithful most of his life, and liked to promote the idea that he had married her for her name.)

He married someone who knew society as he never had, and she married a man—"the small fellow with the big head" as one Montreal banker described him about this time—who knew modern enterprise like few men in the world, and had a limitless faith in his own ability.

To say that he benefited from the marriage by marrying money (as some do) is in the end as pointless as saying that her father approved of the match only when he discovered Max to be a financial genius. (Her parents did not attend the wedding.) When he married Gladys, he was already earning more in a year than most of her other suitors could ever hope to in ten. That, of course, is not suggesting that money was the wand that changed him from Frog to Prince. Many close to Gladys disapproved violently of Max on a more personal level. The man lived in a hotel, and was a wheeler-dealer, for God's sake! What is more, I am sure Max was aware of this. He knew his faults and often embellished them himself. And perhaps he would never have considered taking a wife who could not be a ready benefit.

Still, was it uncommon for a man to benefit from a marriage in that closed society? Herbert Asquith, who would become Liberal prime minister in Great Britain at the start of the First World War and a strong political rival of Max Aitken, had done just that when he married his wife, Violet. In fact, in the genteel society to which many people, and many Canadians, felt that Max shouldn't belong, it was done all the time.

They went to Cuba on their honeymoon, where he worked out a deal to buy a tram line.

IN 1904, John Stairs died at the King Edward Hotel in Toronto, creating another vacuum in Aitken's life, and Max was not made a director of the finance and bond company,

Royal Securities, as he had been promised. Again, he says, he felt betrayed, but there are indications that he did not expect to be made a member of the board. However it went, he inspired more fear and distrust than other men. Perhaps he could not help this.

Still, he was also inconsolable at the death of the man he called "my hero." In private he sought sympathy, ironically enough (or maybe not), from Charles Porter, a music director at the Presbyterian college in Halifax, who, far from giving sympathy, attacked him for thinking he was something more than "an ordinary insurance salesman." It seems to me that Max often relied on stuffy moralizers to assure him he was being good or bright or clever. But once they told him he wasn't being good, he would turn with wrath against them. This, in fact, was something of a constant pattern in his life.

Most in Halifax believed that John F. Stairs had protected his young charge, and now that Stairs was gone, they hoped that Max would flounder badly. In fact, of all the men who had helped him, Stairs had provided the greatest leg up. Yet Max was in many respects the most forward-thinking and aggressive business partner in Stairs's group, and had brought it a good deal of financial success. At the time of Stairs's death, he was in a struggle to save the Scotia Group's

People's Bank of Halifax from being sold to the Bank of Montreal for a bargain-basement price.

That was Max's curse: the juggernaut against him—the hope of much less worthy men that he would fail. ("He was pulled out of the gutter by John Stairs," said one disgruntled businessman about this time.)

So Max left Halifax behind, some time after his marriage, and took up residence in Montreal.

He was on his own again, and by 1908, with the birth of daughter Janet, a young family man. But his older mentors, none of whom were as intelligent as he was, had nonetheless acted as true moral stabilizers on his robust enthusiasms and somewhat delinquent personality. Unfortunately, not only he but others too were soon to realize this.

CHAPTER SEVEN

The Great Canadian Cement Caper and the CPR

Montreal. A great place for a Canadian Scotsman then. A city of lights and ladies, fine dining and moneyed gentlemen. Perhaps he was thinking of never going any farther. This was the top in Canada—and for some reason he never felt comfortable in the States, though he had made financial gains there when he was with Stairs. He made money in Montreal, took over Montreal Trust, and after a time bought out Royal Securities in Halifax, which he and Stairs had set up.

"Royal Securities was me," he stated.

He hired young men as ambitious as he was, like Arthur Nesbitt and Izaak Walton Killam, to handle his Maritimes affairs. (Killam and Nesbitt would become famous financiers in their own right.) Blake Burrill worked for him as manager of the Royal Securities office in Halifax. Aitken was a hard and unreasonable taskmaster. He knew most of the major players in Canada, and associated with many from Boston and beyond. I think there would be little dispute that, in his twenties and thirties, he was at the height of his genius.

Yet he was morally on his own. And this was a bad thing, for Max and morals collided often enough. It seems he had had his fill of those when growing up, and saw the hypocrisy that could lie behind them. This was unfortunate, for his wife, Gladys, was dependent on him for love and protection, and it seemed that the prankster in his personality always came to the fore when she could least afford it emotionally. He felt she nagged and smothered him, and wanted too much attention. They argued over this, and I suspect she was frightened of him (most people were).

So he took his own apartment, again in a hotel, and she returned with Janet, to Halifax. They lived apart for a time—and it would become a standard condition of their marriage. Though never divorced or legally separated, he would live on his own, she at home with the children.

I am sure he believed he was brighter than most men on earth—a very dangerous thing to believe even if one *is* brighter than most men on earth. I am also sure his ruthlessness was in part intellectually based. For once he ascribed nothing to chance or luck; once he realized the limitations of his reverend father, this meant that to be master of his own fate, he must do unsavoury things in order to succeed. For if you think of certain actions, seeing success as your only goal, and do not do them, more fool you!

Yet, if Max was ruthless, there wasn't a parson in the world who could be more generous, even if they had the funds. There is a great story about him at Saint Mary's Hospital in England. He was asked if he could help build a wing on this hospital. He went to visit and, while he was sitting in the cafeteria, he was approached by an elderly lady attendant. She told him that the tea and biscuits were a penny halfpence but, if he couldn't afford it, she would give them to him free. Max was delighted, and wrote a cheque for £63,000 for the hospital wing.

CEMENT IS WHERE he made his initial fortune—and where people who dealt with him say he stole it. Stole is a harsh word. Was he unethical? Most likely, he was—but was he really and truly dishonest? Probably no more so than his adversaries.

In 1909 his finances were basically secure. He was on a roll, and he had a name, even if it was a name that wouldn't recommend him to each and all. (He was refused entrance into an exclusive Montreal business club that year, because of his bad reputation.)

He told his biographer, A.J.P. Taylor, that he set out to buy the English-language *Montreal Gazette*, for which he had once worked as a correspondent. Max said he was stopped by the Bank of Montreal and by the influential board members of the Canadian Pacific Railway, who did much business with the bank. Max was known as a young and brash Conservative financier and industrialist, untrustworthy, impetuous, and shamelessly given to acquiring companies for the purpose of monopoly and merger. This in itself is a psychological red flag to Canadians. The upshot of this was that the influential board of the CPR did not want unsavoury Conservative Max Aitken acquiring the only English-speaking newspaper in Montreal—at that time the one real city in Canada.

But then something very strange happened.

Soon after this event, that very same CPR board needed the merger insight of Max Aitken. Sir Edward Clouston, a man with a profile somewhat like the mustachioed villain in silent films, and president of the Bank of Montreal, enthusiastically put Max's name forward.

So the board members approached Max Aitken, seeking out the same qualities they had rejected just a few months before. They had three cement companies, and they needed his ruthless efficiency to create a merger, which would generate sales, and to sell the stock to the public. As promoter of this merger deal, he would be rewarded with a percentage of the profits from the shares sold.

He was asked by Sir Sandford Fleming, a member of the board of the Canadian Pacific Railway, himself. (Fleming, who would have been eighty at this time, had been the chief engineer in the building of our national railway, the "inventor" of Standard Time, and the main advocate for the telegraph cable between Canada and Australia. Now, late in life, he was to deal with another major challenge, Mr. Max Aitken. It is strange how fate sometimes plays out its hand.)

Yet, as Marchildon explains in his book *Profits and Politics*, there was a very serious devil in the details. Fleming was very close to bankruptcy, and was in a panic to save his reputation. This was something Max Aitken was not told. The price of cement was down, because of the economic crash of 1907, which Aitken had witnessed with alarm. Worse, Fleming's partner in the Western Cement Company, a man named Irvin, had skimmed $500,000 as payment to himself from the company. Fleming had desperately borrowed funds from the Bank of Montreal against the value of the company, and petitioned the CPR for financial help. Now he owed them both hundreds of thousands. But he and Irvin realized that, with the low price of cement and lack of development, a merger of some sort was required to save him. If anyone could pull it off, Max could.

At first the planned merger went well. But Max to his death insisted that he discovered a ruse. One company they wanted to float, Exshaw of Alberta, was bankrupt, and Fleming's partner, Irvin, was also willing to skim money from any unwitting partners, like, as Marchidon states, a pyramid or Ponzi scheme, in which the people in control sell out to those coming in and reap the benefits, leaving the buyers with the debt. This was something Irvin didn't think Max would discover.

As for Exshaw's bankruptcy, Irvin and Fleming hoped to hide this. To keep the bankruptcy from the other cement companies who were joining the merger would be criminal. By its very nature, the merger was dishonest, and Max knew he would be singled out as the force behind a dishonest merger. This is probably why Clouston chose him.

So Max did something reckless and brilliant. He let other cement companies across Canada and in the States know that a great merger was taking place, which would regulate the price and the quality of cement. Over a few months he swamped the Fleming interests by bringing many of the cement companies in Canada into the mix, to create Canada Cement. Max made one of his own investment companies the principal controller of the deal. He used Sandford Fleming's name to give it respectability, while he dwarfed and marginalized the Fleming interests. Then, with Clouston's help, he took over the monopoly himself.

But speaking on Aitken's behalf, I have to say that Max's wiliness does not automatically give Mr. Fleming or Mr. Irvin the sanctity of the higher moral ground.

Finding himself in a precarious position, Aitken had simply turned the tables on those who were prepared to use him. Once on a roll, and seeing a fabulous opportunity to control stock in cement companies that would help reinvigorate the industry, he became the ruthless executor of his own advantage. But is that a terrible thing for a businessman to do? Is it even illogical? Many contend he put the difference between the actual worth and the paper worth of the companies involved in the merger into his own pocket. Others say he bribed Clouston, giving a huge kickback to the president of the Bank of Montreal. My question is pragmatic, I know. Was he the only one who knew Sir Edward Clouston had that bad habit of taking kickbacks? Did any of the CPR board members, who had been acquainted with the president longer and at closer quarters, know? Had they used this flaw themselves, perhaps to stop Max's other ventures, like the *Gazette* purchase in 1909? Max, remember, was the one who was kept out of the business club in Montreal.

From this deal, Max ended up an exceedingly wealthy man. People felt that he had used the old man, Mr. Fleming, atrociously. Although the transactions remain murky on all sides, Fleming was never blamed and Aitken's reputation would never recover.

But the lesson Max took from this cement caper was that he would always and forever be able to leapfrog over his opposition. This in some ways accounted for his erratic springboard approach to other great deals in his life.

They said he would not, could not, come back to Canada. Yet when you are a player of Aitken's wiles, going to England in 1910, to the front row of Empire, who in hell would want to? But at any rate I saw him walking a street in Newcastle in 1958.

CHAPTER EIGHT

English Shores

England then was not the England of today. When Max scampered onto its shores in 1910, his pockets already laden with cash, his abilities fine-tuned, it was still one of the great powers in the world. It was still the greatest empire, at its twilight to be sure, but nevertheless, secure in itself and in all things British. Tolstoy says in *War and Peace* that the assumption was "What was British was proper and right."

A queen had sat on the throne for sixty years and had defined an age, its men and women travelled the globe, and its military still controlled a good part of it. Max Aitken came from one small part of that globe, but his allegiance in so many respects was to Britain, and, in fact, he was a British citizen. It is strange nowadays to think that a boy growing up in Newcastle, New Brunswick, could suddenly find himself running for the British House of Commons.

Ion Benn the British Unionist (Tory) said he was the one to get Max his seat, because he had seen his potential while on a visit to Montreal. It is not really true that he "got Max his seat"—however, he did help him in many ways. He introduced him as a financier from Canada—and, more significantly, he clearly attached a value to this at a time when British financiers thought there was nothing valuable in Canada. As always, it is the fools who block the doors. But it was amazing with what relative ease Max Aitken went through the doors supposedly closed to him.

Max loved the Empire but over time would come to hate many of those who believed they owned it. This would become the principal difficulty in his life, and cause much trouble for him, morally and professionally. For he believed that he, a common boy from Newcastle, was as much a part of the Empire as they. That, in fact, was how the Empire promoted itself. Perhaps the least-known trait in Max was gullibility.

It is old-fashioned now, but then the Empire was lifeblood to many English-speaking Canadians, so it must have been a shock when many of the aristocracy tried to impede Aitken at every step. (It is equally amazing to me how many Canadians cheer that he was impeded.) The idea of him as an outsider would increase with his power and the hope his enemies had that he could be kept forever on the outside.

Tolstoy, in his famous observations on national conceit, said the British were conceited because they came from the greatest Empire on earth, and therefore believed everything that they did must be proper and right. This was still true when Max was a young man. I am sure many British did not think of Canada as anything more than property they (supposedly) owned. How he must have butted his head against them, this colonial with money.

THE FIRST LETTER of introduction he had to this rarified London was to a fellow New Brunswicker, Andrew Bonar Law. (Their museums are now fifty miles apart in the province of New Brunswick.) Bonar Law was born in Rexton, New Brunswick, in 1858, and moved to Scotland when he was sixteen, after his mother's death, to find employment with his family's ironworks. By the time Max arrived, he was a well-established sitting member of the Conservative Party, having first represented Glasgow-Blackfriars and then Dulwich. In pictures he looks a little, at least to me, like Joseph Conrad, who would recently have published *The Secret Agent*, a strangely comic masterpiece that shows a darker aspect of the seething temper of the times.

Law was cool to Max (coming from the opposite side of the Scottish Religious question) and Max felt Law could never succeed because of the "shape of his head"—perhaps the strangest and most comic of all the strange and sometimes comic beliefs Max the pragmatist had. But Law was not immune to the young man's sales ability, and he bought five hundred shares of a stock Max was selling. Max was always selling, and when he went to England the main thing he was selling was himself, wrapped up as manna from Canada. He sold himself the same way as he sold eggs from his hens, or Bennett in Chatham—with too much sauce and not enough meat. You can imagine casually inviting him to visit you at some time in the future, only to discover him standing at your door at eight o'clock the next morning. In fact, Bonar Law once actually had the door locked against him, just like many others before and some after. But he let Max back in—just like many others before and some after.

It did show his ability to keep them, or at least himself, enthused.

Of course, meeting Bonar Law, the boy from Rexton, New Brunswick, who was to become prime minister of Great Britain in 1922, was a pivotal event in Max Aitken's life. Bonar Law would become another older man who would string a tightrope and watch how the little Newcastle imp could don a top hat and twirl a cane while perched upon it.

In fact the friendship between these two New Brunswickers would shape the next twelve years of British politics, first within the ranks of the British Conservative Party and then within the office of the prime minister itself.

It is strange how quickly our man got on in Britain. One forgets that, as a British citizen, and as a millionaire, and with introductions to Bonar Law and other expatriate Canadians, Max Aitken had inroads already ploughed. And amid all this glitter—Henry James was still writing, George V was ascending the throne, young (or youngish) Churchill was conniving for power, there were parties in tuxes and dinner at the club—he must have thought he had landed at the top of the world. In a way he had. It was the London of Piccadilly Circus and Trafalgar Square, of London Bridge and the Thames, of Henry VIII and Elizabeth I, of Chaucer, Shakespeare, and Marlowe, of eighteenth-century scribblers like Sam Johnson and nineteenth-century icons like Charles Dickens, and of political men of only a generation before, like Disraeli and Gladstone. Max, too, wanted to climb to the top of the greasy pole—he was too certain of his destiny not to—but it's hard to know if he wanted the prime ministership. If he had thought Saint John, New Brunswick, was awe-inspiring when he was a boy, look what he'd gotten up to now!

He would never take up permanent residence in Canada again (though on three occasions he would try). He was one of the casualties, not of the cement shenanigans back home (or not just that) so much as of Canada's inability to set a course for itself and keep its brightest and most influential citizens Canadian. In a sense Max was like Canadian silent-film icon Mary Pickford, or fellow New Brunswickers Louis B. Mayer, co-founder of MGM (who was born in Russia but educated in New Brunswick) and 1940s actor Walter Pigeon, or later still, Saint John–born Donald Sutherland. He, like they, had to go where there would be a reasonable chance of becoming a star. However, he would be blamed for this "flaw" of being Canadian—in Britain far more than they were in the States. And Canada and Canadians have treated the memories of these film stars with a reverence our pugnacious newspaper baron never managed to corral. Yet there was no Canadian of the century more influential. Perhaps in a way (shudder to think), a saviour of our way of life. Why is this not remembered? Why is our whole contribution to the world thrown off a cliff to oblivion, and none of us dare say shame?

HE IMMEDIATELY set about making friends and influencing people, and he could do it, because he had boldness and audacity and money on his side. He lived for a kind of social experience and loved the dazzling and impertinent life that the manse back home forbade. At its highest level it was the life Henry James described in novels like *The Wings of the Dove*. It was just as dazzling and every bit as sordid. It was the epitome of the life he dreamed he saw as a child from his window late at night.

He, in fact, had not changed much from the boy counting the hairs on his teacher's moustache. What is amazing is that his rise to power was every bit as startling and as large for a time as Winston Churchill's—or greater, since Churchill was an aristrocrat. William Manchester, in *The Last Lion*, his biography of Winston Churchill, speaking of Churchill's genius, called it a "Zigzag streak of lightning in the brain." It can be safe to say Max Aitken had this as well. In fact it can be safe to say that, for a good seven to ten years, he was as powerful as any man in Britain, which made him as influential as any man in Europe. And most of this occurred before he was forty.

CHAPTER NINE

Knighthood

So the wheeler-dealer comes to England, meets associates of Bonar Law, and is introduced as a Conservative financier from Canada. He buys Rolls-Royce—not a car, as one of my acquaintances thought when I told him of Max's influence in 1910, but the company.

Cars were new, and Max loved new. (The manse had one of the first telephones in Newcastle, when Aitken was a boy; perhaps it was then that his fascination with new gadgetry took hold.) He was always seduced by the idea of invention. Perhaps he was drawn to the idea that we could control, by invention, the world itself. It is really a materialistic ideal—and Max embraced this from the first time he stepped from his door and saw an electric light.

Of course, he soon became bored and impatient with Rolls-Royce, just as he was bored and impatient with so much in his life, with the houses he bought and the women he bedded. He was a good starter, A.J.P. Taylor states about his eclectic personality, but "he was not a sticker." And as far as production was concerned, he had an assembly-line mentality if ever there was one. Rolls-Royce did not. It had the rather British idea that, if you wanted something made well, you must wait for it—especially if there were only a few to be sold.

He sold Rolls-Royce to an American. (We, that is the Western world, would be glad in 1940 that Max had an in with Rolls-Royce.)

One of the members of the board of Rolls-Royce was Baron (later Viscount) Northcliffe, the "Press Lord," who owned *The Times*. He didn't think Max would be at all interested in newspapers, but he liked to quote him in his. Aitken was always good for a quote about politics. Max was an anti-tariff bulldog, the sort of eccentric papers like, for they say outrageous things, a visionary Empire loyalist who screamed for preferential treatment between the colonies and Britain.

The country had been in the throes of this "Imperial Preference" debate (that is, Free Trade among Britain and her colonies) for a number of years, and Max wanted this desperately. This is probably how he got to know a man who was, for a time, one of his staunchest friends in Great Britain, the famous writer Rudyard Kipling, who held the same views. One was from the boonies of Canada, one was from the boonies of India, and how they got on trying to relay to Britain the importance of her destiny.

At this time the cement fiasco was breaking news in Canada. Max, safely in England, was being vilified for betrayal and common malfeasance. I think he believed that he could succeed his way out of a bad reputation. He had the new Conservative prime minister of Canada, Robert Borden, on his side, willing to stop a parliamentary investigation. His old friend Bennett was investigating Fleming's partner, Irvin, and discovering him to be not much more than a common thief. But as far as improving his reputation, Max, over his long career, would be only partially successful.

During this time, he was still trying to run his companies from Britain, and was doing business in Calgary with Bennett, setting up a hydroelectric plant for that city, and also creating a grain-transport facility with both Bennett and his old pal Clouston. Yet, as Gregory Marchildon indicates, over the next few years Max would be slowly forced to let go of his economic interests in the Caribbean, and even Royal Securities would be taken over and run by Izaak Walton Killam. So, whatever his feelings, Max's future rested where he was.

He knew this. So, soon after arriving in Britain, he was giving donations to the British Tory party, and in 1911, was knighted during the coronation of King George V.

Sir Max decided he would become a politician. In doing so, he would attract accusations once again—this time of political intrigue.

MANY WILL SAY that his friendship with Bonar Law was all political calculation on Max's part, and as soon as a House of Commons seat was available, at Ashton-under-Lyne, he rushed to Law's house and begged for the candidacy. As A.J.P. Taylor relates, he actually said, like a little boy, "What about me? Why can't I run?" and was rewarded by being given the chance. Some people say he was simply at Bonar Law's house at the most opportune time, and Bonar Law shrugged and said, "Okay. I'll see what I can do for you."

Be that as it may, he truly cared for Bonar Law (and was much more helpful to him than Law was to Max), and was beyond doubt the most instrumental force in Bonar Law's political career. I also think that if Bonar Law was, as is claimed almost happily by some in Canada, the least effective British prime minister, as a leader of the opposition Conservative Party, Law's abilities were profound. Max was the horse Bonar Law rode, and tried to rein in.

So, by 1912, Sir Max Aitken was seeking office in Britain. He ran his own campaign for Ashton-under-Lyne with his wife Gladys as beautiful decoy, spending as much money as the seat warranted. He told a local reporter to go easy on him because he had been in politics only a week. That statement in itself is courageous, for it appeals to anyone with a sense of humour. It shows his understanding of what people wanted, and they wanted, at least for now, the bright new voice from Canada (even though they hated his Miramichi accent and the way he pronounced the names of their towns). He helped things along by having nice things written about him in Canadian papers, and then republished in local Ashton ones—a good enough ploy if one dares use it.

The trade unions went for him, even though they recognized that he made promises whether or not he had any idea of their import. Sounds like the Bennett campaign of fifteen years before. Or in fact most campaigns of today. He won the seat by 196 votes.

Now he was in, as a Tory, and immediately became friends with Winston Churchill and David Lloyd George— two radical Liberals (Churchill, of course, would later become a Conservative).

Bonar Law was jealous of these new friendships of Max's— and suspicious of their political stripes. He felt betrayed. All his life, Max would do infuriating things like this. But Aitken liked Lloyd George and Churchill in spite of their political stripes—and besides, Churchill was Churchill, one of the most famous names in Britain, who had chronicled his true heroics in the Boer War, and Aitken needed to meet him.

However, what is less known is that, at this point, Aitken suddenly went back home—to Newcastle, New Brunswick. He was wined and dined as a great success and was asked to run as a Conservative for Northumberland County, where Newcastle was the shire town. He thought about it but decided against it. He went back to England. What caused this trip?

This was one of three trips he would make back to Canada, hoping to settle at home. All three times he realized, like someone does with an unrequited love, that it is never to be. There is a picture of him as an old man, walking a lane in New Brunswick, with his limousine a hundred yards behind him—like a child searching for something he lost along the way.

CHAPTER TEN

Cherkley as a Front for Family Life

When he got back to England, he left his house in London and bought Cherkley, an estate twenty miles outside the city in Surrey, and Gladys and Rudyard Kipling's wife got down to the job of remodelling it. Cherkley in fact looked something like a big square manse, but it had its moments, and was to become palatial and splendid. This was perhaps Gladys Aitken's happiest year, with true friends helping her in her new home, young children—Janet, John William (called Max), and Peter—and an exceedingly popular (for the moment) husband. There would be parties and love and laughter—for a while. Her life would never be this content again. Max liked to think—and it must have been just a whim—that he could be something of a country squire. He would leave the rat race behind, and live with his brood on the estate. It lasted a month. Then he crept back to London, returning to Cherkley only on the weekends.

THOUGH HE WAS only a backbencher, because he was an intimate of Bonar Law he was all of a sudden a major player. People were frightened of Max Aitken, as they are of any force of nature, and many wanted to reduce his influence to remove their fear. He was also inexhaustibly bright, and curious enough about others to make friends easily. But he could be as deadly as a snake with venom if thwarted. He continued in finance, both in Canada and England, bought a bank in Britain, and had a fondness for gambling in Monte Carlo.

He stayed in London to see what was happening in the political theatre. Once again, he was not in Gladys's life, though she struggled to make a life for them all. Now she was in a foreign land, with her children. He would come back and forth, but it was like it always was, and always would be; there was always a hotel, where he could stay away. He would dress to go out to dine at night, at the gayest spots in town, alone. There were always other women. And he did not chastise himself for this, until it was too late.

Aitken came to England and to the government in a time of real class upheaval. The world was changing. The Conservative (or, as it was also called up until the First World War, the Unionist) Party, ostensibly the party of the upper classes, the party he belonged to, was in disarray; the Irish were pressing for Home Rule; the power of the establishment, in the guise of the fuddy-duddy House of Lords, was being challenged by people like the radical Liberal cabinet minister David Lloyd George; radicalism was sweeping the rank and file of British Labour, too. There were anarchists, nihilists, and Fenians. Women were calling for a voice in decision-making. There were marches and protests in the street. There was also a smell of war on the wind. All of this created divisions and fear and opportunity. Yes, it was the top of the world, and it spun like a top that might tumble on its side.

Max longed to be a player in the Conservative ranks in England. It was part of his nature to want to rule, or at the very least to belong with those who did. The famous picture of him walking side by side with Churchill on the HMS *Prince of Wales* in 1941 was no accident. Don't think that, just because he wanted to be there, he was not needed by those he walked beside.

Still, not everyone was at ease with him. There was much talk about and against him by very famous British politicians, who hoped to stop him before he became too powerful. He was often the subject of gossip. His lax moral form was constantly whispered about.

There were flaws in his registry others were straining to see. They were trying to place him—somewhere where he wouldn't be a threat. Asquith, the British Liberal prime minister, distrusted him immensely, and told Churchill so in 1911, writing, of Max becoming a commissioner of trade, "Aitken is quite impossible, his Canadian record is of the shadiest." He was a charlatan and an upstart. They hated the idea of his wealth, and how he waded through the scene like a bull in a china shop. He could foresee trouble, he just couldn't pinpoint exactly where it was. He was also a bounder. A common adulterer.

Still I ask, if he had stayed at Cherkley, had dinner with Gladys, spoken to the nanny about his children, would the world have been the better for it? Could one believe his marriage would have been?

CHAPTER ELEVEN

Law Becomes
Conservative Leader

For much of Aitken's life, he was propelled or driven to succeed on the back of failure. He was also the kind of man who liked to create division. This is why he had in some circles such a bad reputation and was so unpopular. He revelled in division, and some say he revelled in his own bad press. There were probably reasons for this that were caused as much by the forces aligned against him as by something within himself.

In 1912, Arthur Balfour, the ageing leader of Britain's Conservative Party, found himself head of an Opposition mired in unpopularity. Balfour, another Scotsman, was an intellectual (Eton and Cambridge) and had actually made something of a name for himself with a book of philosophy, *Defense of Philosophic Doubt*, published in 1889. He was a lifelong bachelor, had come up under former prime minister the Marquis of Salisbury (a man of the nineteenth century), and was now part of the old guard. According to Liberals like Prime Minister Asquith and David Lloyd George, he was relying on the hated aristocratic House of Lords for his main political support. The radical wing of the Liberal Party, headed by Lloyd George, was ostensibly for the common man, and wanted to weaken the power of this same muddling House of Lords once and for all.

When a bill was passed to contravene the power of the Lords, and Balfour, as Opposition leader, lost the Conservative fight against this bill, he was forced by his own party, to step down.

Aitken did not care much for the House of Lords either. Even if he was a Conservative and the House of Lords was a mainstay of Conservatism, he was still too much of a Canadian. One of the problems Max had was subtle enough. How could he be a Conservative, if he came, as he said, from poverty in Canada? That is, people constantly equate Conservatism not with values but with property, especially if they themselves are liberal or socialist, propertied or not.

With Balfour gone, Max helped persuade his friend Bonar Law to run for the leadership of the Conservative Party. He also persuaded Bonar Law to let him, Max Aitken, handle the campaign. For Max knew how to handle things when things got unsavoury. For Bonar Law, it was perhaps the best thing to happen to his political career. Law's sister once complained to Law about this "awful man" Aitken, and Bonar Law supposedly said: "Mary, allow me to love him."

The Conservative leadership of Great Britain would never have gone to the man from Rexton, New Brunswick, if Max Aitken from Newcastle, New Brunswick, hadn't been one of the main players behind the scenes. He sized up the opposition and saw them to be the kind of mediocrities he had dealt with before. Max very likely had little respect for them and always, as a "cat who walked alone," wanted to prove himself against them.

In the beginning, a Mr. Walter Long and Austin Chamberlain were running neck and neck against one another for the Unionist (Conservative) Party leadership. Though many Unionists of the time lamented that both candidates left much to be desired, the name Chamberlain is synonymous with British politics. Austin Chamberlain, older brother of the future prime minister Neville Chamberlain (1937–1940), who was to cave in to Hitler at Munich, had been chancellor of the exchequer under Prime Minister Arthur Balfour. His pictures, as those of his brother Neville, make me think of an austere nineteenth-century butler. He was from one of the most powerful Conservative families in the realm, and probably would have won, had not Sir Max Aitken himself stepped in, convinced Law, who was widely thought to be clear-thinking and practical, to run—and then taken the helm of Bonar Law's campaign.

Aitken's strategy was simple enough. He had Bonar Law's supporters first back Long, then shift en masse to Chamberlain, then back to Long—like passengers rushing from one side of a sightseeing ship to the other. Finally the party realized that Bonar Law, who could so sway the leadership race, must be their new leader, as the great compromise that many wanted in the first place. Sir Max Aitken's hands were all over this. So, I am sure, was his money. Like a behind-the-scenes conjuror, he always ran boards without belonging to them. This is why I never took seriously the contention that he aspired to the prime ministership. He was much better at back-room stuff. In this he was not unlike another New Brunswicker, of my father's generation, Dalton Camp.

Still, back in 1912, many of the crème de la crème of the British Conservative Party felt they had been forced into this compromise by this man from away, and they would never forget the sting. They would never forget Max's large head and moccasin mouth, grinning at them, like a man who has just put them in checkmate. Max was already disliked by the Liberals. So we will see, in the next few years, how both Liberals and Conservatives formed an unspoken British-born, Eton-educated coalition against him—one that he didn't see coming until it was too late.

Max had had great moments already, but there were flaws and weaknesses that his enemies were straining to see. And some of these enemies were as cunning . . . well, as cunning as his good friend, Welsh-born radical Liberal David Lloyd George himself.

CHAPTER TWELVE

War

> "I'm a friend of old Lloyd George
> And George is a friend of me
> Together we will go
> Marching to Victory!"

So went the song.

Just for sheer stupidity, baseness, governmental pomposity, upper-class egomania, and false morality, no other war approaches the war of 1914–1918. It came out of a welter of snubs and threats and bluster, and ended wiping out an entire generation, and at least four monarchies. So quickly did it come that Bonar Law himself, head of the Conservative Party of Great Britain in 1914, had to explain why his own Scottish ironworks were still selling steel for German battleships. The secretary (and second wife) of Liberal cabinet minister David Lloyd George, Frances Stevenson, was so worried about Liberal defections if Prime Minister Asquith supported going to war on the side of France and Russia without real provocation, that, as she wrote, she prayed every night for Germany to invade Belgium to give England a "just" cause. We can see that Lloyd George's radicalism and precious fight for the common man, the "little English," who would end up doing most of the fighting, must have contained at least a little self-interested power-seeking in the end.

Sir Max Aitken did not want war, and was surprised that so many of his colleagues did. (In fact this is a central point of Aitken's life, and perhaps it came from the manse: he never wanted war—except on a personal level.)

But he was also aware of the fact that the sitting Liberal government might have to form a coalition with the Tory Opposition in order to last through this war. And, being Max, he was content to try and get this worked out, for his and Bonar Law's benefit. That a coalition would increase Bonar Law's power was unquestionable—and Sir Max was a dear, dear friend and confidant of Bonar Law.

The Liberal Winston Churchill actually wanted and promoted a coalition government in early August 1914. He did this for one reason: in case of a revolt against the war within his own Liberal Party. All of this, of course, delighted Max.

For the first time in a few years, Max, who perhaps thought little of his duties as an MP, spent some of his time in the House of Commons, dining with both Liberal and

Tory members. But once Germany did invade Belgium, the die was cast, the non-intervention revolt within the Liberal ranks was thwarted, and a coalition became unnecessary (for the moment).

Rudyard Kipling wrote to Aitken, claiming it was the end of civilized life. Max, it was said, reassured him with £50 in gold, a sack of flour, and a ham. The trouble with a great imagination, as Conrad wrote in *Lord Jim*, is that it can play havoc with your nerves.

Aitken fell out of favour with his Tory party in September 1914, and with Kipling soon after, over what he considered foolish hysterics over Irish Home Rule, which did not matter with a major war near their shores. (He supported Home Rule for all of Ireland, while Law, and most in the House of Lords, wanted Ulster excluded.) Aitken and Bonar Law had a bitter argument over this, and Max left for Canada. He even thought of staying and becoming a sitting member for Northumberland County once again. Once again he wanted to go back to his roots and live life in a simpler way.

He was only persuaded to go back to Great Britain as the voice for Canada, and to create the Canadian War Records Office—and he ended up doing this better than anyone ever could. He was so successful that the British High Command complained by 1915 that it seemed to the world that Canada was in every battle. (Well, they were in enough.)

Max visited the Front as a lieutenant-colonel, for he was preparing to write a book about the Canadians. In a picture I have seen, he looks like an enthusiastic schoolboy ready to see a chemist's lab explode. He may have been kept out of harm's way, but if he was anywhere close to the Front, that may have been impossible. He could well have gone to the Front just after Churchill visited, for Max was an enthusiastic imitator of others. All his life he imitated those who assumed they were his betters, even if he knew in most ways they weren't. Winston Churchill, of course, was one exception to this rule. Still, if Winston went, he would go too. When Winston had a painting done by Graham Sutherland in the 1950s, Max had one done as well. Stanley Baldwin (Conservative prime minister of Great Britain in the 1920s and 1930s) had a fine player piano at 10 Downing Street. In Max's museum in Newcastle, New Brunswick, one sits. Hey, my boys, this is what the orphan does.

BACK IN ENGLAND, Max now and again entertained friends at Cherkley. On many a weekend there was a party, in the good old-fashioned Miramichi tradition. I don't know if they all sat in the kitchen, but the guest book was filled. Max had other interests too, besides business and politics. He set up house in apartments in the neighbourhood called The Temple, closer to town, and then, closer still, in Hyde Park, a few blocks from Opposition leader Bonar Law.

From here he kept his eye on the shifting politics of the time and tried with some measure of success to influence events. He had many lady friends, seduced by his money, his fame and power, his narcissism, and his pretended devil-may-care attitude. For almost a year he stayed away from his family. And it was at his apartment in The Temple that his wife and children, coming to visit him one day, found him in bed with a well-known lady. These intrigues would in time help to kill his wife, and in the end turned his daughter's love to hatred.

Max has been criticized for a great many things. He has been accused of theft and being a womanizer. Theft maybe not; womanizer, of course. He bedded many. A moral lapse certainly, but why such reaction to the man? The last thing he pretended to was sainthood. In fact, he dabbled in that moral ambiguity so fashionable in our politics and literature and culture of today. Clementine Churchill, one of the women who hated him (which I always thought showed her distinct lack of imagination), had an affair herself, which most people neglect to mention, or tacitly approve.

Max did not fare as well with that kind of shoddy public opinion. I for one am not saying that he should have. But so much of this was tossed his way by a society in which mores were corrupt and understood to be. The reputation of David Lloyd George, the brilliant Liberal radical who became prime minister of Britain in 1916, fares much better, though he demonstrated the same incontinence. In one letter, Lloyd George writes that Max had the blood of broken Commandments on his hands, but Lloyd George was dubbed "the Goat" by others in the House, and had a man in his employ who would pay off women who had been offended by his sometimes overt advances.

BUT AT THIS TIME, on those grey, rainy, and tragic days, with huge dreadnoughts in the English Channel, Max was truly the main connection between the two political parties in Great Britain. Yes, apart from champagne and women and making sure the contributions of Canadians in the war effort were recognized around the world, he would do another merger. As his friend H.G. Wells, writer of *The War of the Worlds* and *The Time Machine*, said, "When Max dies, he will be kicked out of paradise for trying to set up a merger between heaven and hell." Of course the war was a terrible hell, and by 1915 this is exactly what he was trying to do.

CHAPTER THIRTEEN

The Making of Prime Minister David Lloyd George

Let's go back to the second decade of the last century for a moment.

Asquith's Liberals were in power. In May 1915 they were reeling from the resignation of Sea Lord Fisher because of his dispute with Winston Churchill, First Lord of the Admiralty (the political position in the Navy), over the sinking of the battleship *Goliath* in the Dardanelles (it was not a huge battleship, but it was the straw that broke the camel's back) and the slaughter of the Australians at Gallipoli. This all happened during the Dardanelles campaign. Churchill had conceived of the plan to take the strait off Turkey, hoping to capture Constantinople and maintain a rearguard action against the enemy, the Germans and Austrians, and the Turks. This caper ended with the loss of a quarter of a million men, and caused the resignation of Sea Lord Fisher and the subsequent firing (if we can call it that) of Churchill.

Losing Sea Lord Fisher over his dispute with an extremely unpopular Winston Churchill was a desperate blow to the Liberal government. Fisher was perhaps the greatest naval officer since Nelson, and had served the British with distinction for almost fifty years. He had masterminded the modernization of the British naval fleet in the early part of the twentieth century, by promoting the building of both submarines and battleships.

But really, by early 1916 there was no way to buoy up the Liberal government of Asquith except with Tory help. Now a coalition would *have* to be formed—that is, a merger. And Max Aitken from Newcastle, New Brunswick, merger-maker extraordinaire, was there.

Here were the principal players in 1916: Asquith, the prime minister (Liberal); Churchill, First Lord of the Admiralty (disgraced Liberal); Fisher, First Sea Lord (resigned); Kitchener, minister of war for Asquith, deceased (the victim of a mine on his way to Russia); Lloyd George, chancellor of the exchequer and top Liberal cabinet minister; Bonar Law, leader of the Conservative Party; Austin Chamberlain, top Tory member; Sir Max Aitken, Tory MP for Ashton-under-Lyne.

MAX AITKEN, as well as many others, was politically astute enough to know that an election during the war would not favour a change in government. Therefore, the best possible solution was for a coalition government, which would for the time being keep Asquith and the Liberals in power but would give the Tories—that is Bonar Law—a strong representation within the war cabinet. And as Bonar Law's friend and confidant, he would tag along. This is what Max hoped for—to be a tag-along into the cabinet.

A.J.P. Taylor states that Aitken wanted Bonar Law to have close to equal authority with the prime minister. Churchill, who had wanted the coalition in 1914, did not want it now for personal reasons. He desperately feared he would lose any personal power if a coalition were formed. The political climate had turned completely against him.

Max was not totally blind to his own position (he never was) and wanted power for himself. That's why he made mergers in the first place. Ask the board of the CPR.

The coalition was formed, and it marked the political death knell for both Churchill (for the moment) and Asquith. Displeasure in the Liberal ranks over the handling of the war threatened to turn into open revolt. Churchill went to the trenches in France, where he stayed for some weeks, facing extreme danger and discomfort.

In December 1916, Asquith resigned, to allow for a new prime minister. Max again wanted Bonar Law in the position. Max, as Taylor states, was now living at the Hyde Park Hotel, in an intimate setting where he could entertain privately, and he was seeing Bonar Law on almost a daily basis.

Bonar Law said no, he could not be prime minister. For one thing it would mean a change in party colours at the helm of the wartime government. Second, Law was always a reluctant combatant. These were desperate times, and perhaps he was frightened of failure. They needed a sitting Liberal to take the reins of a coalition government, and that Liberal would be David Lloyd George. In every meeting that Aitken had had with Bonar Law and others, from mid-1915 forward, David Lloyd George had been present and had posed as Aitken's friend. At that time their offices were two doors from one another. Lloyd George had made himself indispensable to the Tories, while pretending to be Asquith's right-hand man.

"We cannot possibly do without Lloyd George," Law supposedly said to Max Aitken early in 1916. So Lloyd George it was. This was Max Aitken's greatest merger, yet he got someone he did not want.

Of course, what was at stake in this 1916 coalition was essentially the entire war effort, the fight against Germany.

If the government couldn't command a united front, how could it direct troops in the field—which even in the best-case scenario were being slaughtered at an unprecedented rate? (For instance, trench warfare caused so many men to be horrifically wounded in the face between 1914 and 1918 that it marked the beginning of plastic surgery.)

If we look closely at the British government crisis of 1916, we can see one of Max's major flaws, one that could and would be seen with any perceived opportunity: his eagerness to do good for someone who perhaps had less talent than he did. He did it for people in Canada, like R.B. Bennett, and he did it for people in England, like Bonar Law. I believe it was in its own way a kind of rarified altruism, by which he hoped to gain the gratitude of older men. But there was another important reason. Max himself had no centre point, no true compass, no sense of moral equilibrium. Unless he was an influence behind the scenes, he would fail. He knew this, and I think Lloyd George did as well.

When Asquith resigned in December 1916, Max backed David Lloyd George, and was as instrumental as most in having him made prime minister.

Max Aitken sought one portfolio, minister of trade. And, Peter Howard states, he believed that Lloyd George had not only promised him this, but owed him this much for his work behind the scenes.

David Lloyd George is a fascinating figure in British politics. A Welshman, born in 1863, he was a great speaker, and at twenty-seven he was the youngest man from Wales ever elected to the House. He learned radical politics on his uncle's knee and was for land reform, the lessening or even obliteration of the hated and dithering House of Lords, women's rights, union rights, and the rights of the "Little English," the tradesmen and shop owners and factory workers who made up much of English society and had been frozen out of real policy-making for centuries. It was to them he owed much of his power.

He was handsome and sometimes hypocritical, but his brilliance cannot be underestimated. Perhaps the one person he feared, strangely enough, was the old curmudgeon Canadian Scotsman Bonar Law. But he seemed able to read Max Aitken, or at any rate knew how to use Max's tremendous ambition against him.

When Lloyd George became prime minister in 1916, Max was convinced he would be made minister of trade.

He had not the slightest inkling that this would not be the case when he spoke to his wife Gladys in Cherkley by telephone from London. He told Gladys he would resign his seat, re-offer for his seat, and be re-elected (the standard obligation in Britain when you are about to become a minister of trade). I believe this was perhaps the closest Max ever came to dividing twenty-five cents into three. Becoming trade minister was everything and it seemed the war was, to him, beside the point.

In a few short weeks he would be out of power, and finished forever as a true politico. For a man who understood human nature and was able to think three steps ahead, Max truly did not see it coming. In a way I am sure many other people did. Many were champing at the bit for revenge, and it was a set-up as deft as the attack on Caesar at the Senate. Certainly the Conservatives, led by Austin and Neville Chamberlain, as well as Mr. Long, were willing to stab. So were many of the Liberals, like former prime minister Asquith, who disliked Max intensely. Perhaps even Max's budding friend Churchill knew, maybe even had a hand in it, and said nothing to warn him; nor could he do anything at that moment to help him. Worse, where was Bonar Law? Law was actually now the second-most-powerful man in the British wartime cabinet, and with his new power he could have insisted that Aitken be there. He did not.

Jenkins in his one-volume biography of Churchill states that what Lloyd George managed to do to Max Aitken he would never have attempted to do to Churchill. But this doesn't speak to Aiken's flaw, so much as his solitude. (Jenkins does not understand this, and thinks the advantage lay in Churchill's political expertise.) That is, there was a certain limit placed on what one might attempt to do to a Churchill, whose family roots, duty, and privilege went back four centuries.

As distrusted as Churchill was, by December 1916 Aitken was also. But no one could really touch Churchill. (In fact, disliked or not, he was brought back into cabinet late in 1917.) Also, Lloyd George was fighting his own public-relations battle at this time. Many were saying he had stabbed his own prime minister, Asquith, in the back and had made an alliance with the Conservatives to get Asquith's job. So, to hand Conservative strategy-boy Sir Max Aitken a portfolio plum would be tantamount to admitting to something he himself was busy trying to deny in the papers. Asquith, in his last week at 10 Downing Street, said Lloyd George was loyal. So David Lloyd George had to at least appear to be. Max saw none of this coming.

But what is significant here is what he was offered instead by David Lloyd George.

CHAPTER FOURTEEN

On Shaky Ground

Thinking he would be offered the minister of trade position, Sir Max Aitken resigned his seat on a cloudless day and sent his faithful wife, Gladys, to campaign on his behalf for re-election, in Ashton-under-Lyne. (She was prettier and had far more class.) Then he found out that newly elected Prime Minister Lloyd George would not back him for the trade portfolio. This was humiliating indeed, for why then did he resign? And, more significantly, why hadn't anyone (including his friends) told him before he resigned that what he dreamed of was not to be?

If they had told him, he wouldn't have resigned and could have still held his seat! But it was a gambit by Liberal prime minister Lloyd George, along with Tory men of high rank, to put him out of power for good. All of a sudden Aitken smelled a rat. He was in a terrible position and too late he realized it.

Aitken's desperate humiliation was to be reinforced when a request came from the prime minister's office later in the week that Aitken relinquish any claim on his recently vacated seat to Albert Stanley, whom the coalition wanted as trade minister.

This was an official request, coming from the coalition government, and therefore not only from the Liberals but from his own Conservative Party. The request was delivered by Bonar Law. And it was done with the callous intimation that Max had done little to deserve more, and would himself know this and be gracious. "They think you have flown too high," was all Bonar Law could say. I think the worst of it is to be slain by the incompetence or indifference of your friends. And it must have hurt deeply.

So, what did they offer him, to make up for the loss of the trade portfolio? A place in the dithering, pompous House of Lords, the very institution that Prime Minister David Lloyd George hated and had tried to destroy! Any power it had once had wielded had been considerably reduced by 1911 by George's Liberal Party. This was cynicism and disrespect at its highest level, adding insult to injury to a man, Max Aitken, who had helped him. It was done by Lloyd George in order to conceal that help and insinuate loyalty to Asquith, the former boss he had just gleefully replaced. (From this point until David Lloyd George's defeat in 1922, the Liberal Party was split in two—and members were called either Asquithians or Georgians.)

As far as the public was concerned, Max seemed to have taken the lordship already, for his seat was up for re-offer.

No friend came with a solution. There was no way to save face, except to accept what was offered or fight for the seat on his own. If he considered fighting on his own, he understood his chances of losing his vacated seat were very large; the entire coalition would in fact be against him. If he became a lord, he could readily save face, not only in England, but in Canada, by saying he had resigned his seat to take the position.

Max had little alternative, and believed, taking the good with the bad, that he could make it up later in his career. This was never to be.

He wanted to take the name Lord Miramichi, but Rudyard Kipling convinced him no one would ever be able to pronounce it (this was borne out later by Queen Elizabeth, who couldn't pronounce the name the one time she attempted it). So, it was Lord Beaverbrook. From here on out he would be known by a name he had never intended, because, up until the moment, it had not been foreseen, yet, the very name would become synonymous to many with a career that had been bought or politicked for.

So he would fight them all. He would isolate himself to do so. He would become the scapegoat. He would be vilified. Yet he would fight. If there was ever a moment when he turned into what the British pictured him to be, this was it.

Many of Max Aitken's enemies present and future did not know just how high he might have gone in the world that spread out before him in 1917. Or perhaps they did know and were afraid.

CHAPTER FIFTEEN

The Press Baron Alley Fighter

He drank, but he was not what we call a falling-down drunk. He partied, and gambled, and lost himself in the arms of splendid women. He licked his wounds with sensual comfort and brandy. He had money to last ten lifetimes. He bought mechanical gadgets that were new, and that he had seen in the houses of the powerful. He moped about, pretending to be happy. But he needed a new weapon to fight them. And so he went back to his first love.

Newspapers.

Newspapers? Well that is the one place where the little bugger could "catch the conscience of the King," to quote Hamlet. He had been writing off and on for papers since he was eleven, and at times the last thing he had been was discreet. He knew how to use newspapers, how to "write a lead," as they say. And he was good at controversy. In fact, whether he liked it or not, since the cement fiasco, "controversy" had become his middle name.

It has been said that he bought the *Daily Express* in 1916 to help bring down Asquith's Liberal government and force the wartime coalition in order to help Bonar Law become prime minister. That may be far-fetched, but he probably did decide that his own world view needed some publicity.

Max was once asked by Lord Northcliffe, also a powerful press baron, how much money he had.

"I have five million," Max said (by which he meant £5 million, which was somewhat more than $20 million Canadian in those days).

"Then you will spend it all on that paper," Northcliffe cautioned, and probably scoffed.

This wasn't to be the case. The bold little fellow went forward with his newspaper, so that, by the end of the 1920s, the *Daily Express* (along with its sister papers, the London *Evening Standard* and the *Sunday Express*) would be the most read, most hated, most cherished paper in the realm. At its height it had a circulation of over three million, and for a long while was also the most read newspaper in the *world*. Beaverbrook had much to do with making it so. He never made it to the Admiralty, but he was called, even by detractors, "the First Lord of Fleet Street." Most of the men he worked with were outsiders like himself. Many were Canadian.

He was creating what would become an entirely new kind of paper, one which could be considered the start of the tabloid press. Like so many of these papers, it was hated by people who never read it. It was called "middle class" by his former colleagues, which was a snub synonymous with "trailer trash" today. Max wrote for it for many years, and became a real working editor.

What made it successful? He, more than his competitors, knew what people wanted. Max Aitken's new newspaper featured, as Peter Howard tells us, a woman's section (the first paper to do so), a crossword puzzle (the first paper to do so), Alfred Bestall's Rupert Bear cartoons, and satirical cartoons by Carl Giles. He was generous to his employees and compensated his workers better than most of the left-wing papers whose owners hated him for his money.

He was, of course, an imperialist, a conservative, and a businessman—all of which seem tainted now. No one made more fun of him than novelist Evelyn Waugh, because, as far as Waugh was concerned, a colonial like Max did not have a right to have money. Yes, it was very bad form. So he was Lord Copper in Waugh's novel *Scoop*. H.G. Wells based a character on him as well: Sir Bussy Woodcock. When Max approached him about it, Wells said: "I needed a character who could think for himself and was able to earn his own money. You are the only person in London I know who can do both!"

Considering how Churchill handled money, and almost went bankrupt doing so, and how most of Max's acquaintances inherited their money, it seemed true.

The famous novelist Rebecca West also created a character based on him. And Rebecca West loved him, had an affair with him, and wanted to marry him. It did not happen.

His paper was right wing of course, and would be viewed harshly by anyone addicted to the kind of status quo papers of the Canadian left today. Aitken was in a fight against rival papers and wasn't beyond using titillation to sell, though I know he would blanch at what is allowed today— say, the bum shot of Chancellor Angela Merkel of Germany. People might say he helped to cause this. But no more than others. Very few litmus tests for taste or decorum are done. Newspapermen are in many ways treacherous rascals, and the game is played on a daily basis. They are sometimes the last to consider personal ethics, and the first to howl in moral outrage if their noses are tweaked by censure. Not that novelists are any better. Novelists simply get you over the long haul. Newspapermen and newspaperwomen have a different kind of venom. Max surely had it. He was also a tit-for-tat kind of guy, and why shouldn't he be? He never had tenure. What he had he had by his own brains. Tit-for-tat was the only method he knew. And tit-for-tat is, in fact, what did him in eventually. It seems once the dust settled, and he realized what had happened, he could not rest as long as David Lloyd George was in power.

THERE WAS A WAR ON, and Max was still in the thick of government. He was a propagandist for Canadian efforts (as mentioned, his title was Canadian War Representative) to such a degree that he was acting almost as High Commissioner for Canada—though Canada already had one. Besides entertaining in his Hyde Park Hotel chambers, he had time to write a three-volume collection called *Canada in Flanders*, and more than any of his Canadian detractors (ever), he made sure that Canadian stories and contributions to the war effort were known and published in British papers. If he embellished, good for him. So little about us had ever been embellished before, or was after.

The Canadian government had put him in charge of creating the Canadian War Records Office in London in 1915. He wisely used some of the funds he was allotted to commission paintings of battles fought by Canadian troops—like Vimy Ridge and Ypres—by painters like Augustus John (who today is famous for painting portraits of poets like Yeats and Dylan Thomas) and Wyndham Lewis (a man who had connections with, and spent time in, Canada). These paintings, which are some of the first to show the real face of war, are startling in their depiction of what battle actually looked like, and it is a great credit to Beaverbrook that some say this effort helped develop modern Canadian art. This is something for which he gets very little or no credit now, and which no one at the time, besides him, thought of doing.

Toward the end of the war, Lloyd George's government made him minister of propaganda, which Max renamed subtly enough minister of information. He was offered this position, in my mind, because Lloyd George feared Max's paper and its influence if it turned against him.

But let us ask this. Why was he made minister of propaganda? Because it was an unsavoury position—think of Hitler's minister of propaganda. It allowed others, who had already heard he was unsavoury, to believe he fit the image they wanted to give him. Did Max know this? Well, he did change the name to minister of information.

Max did this job with zeal, but of course he did not have the free hand he had had when dealing with Canadian command. And, after Max brought Lord Northcliffe of *The Times* on board, some in the House of Commons roared foul that two newspaper barons with ties to the government were allowed to embellish the progress of the war. Lord Salisbury (the son of the former prime minister) stated that Max Aitken was a very wicked man.

Asked to prove it, he simply said: "Oh, just ask anyone in Canada."

"Lord Salisbury is a vile landowner—ask any one of his tenants," Max quipped.

But this is the kind of admonition he had to face, and he began to fight back as ruthlessly as he could. And, I might add, why shouldn't he?

THERE ARE PICTURES of him at spas with his children, Peter and Max, and later on, looking out over seacoast resorts by himself or attended by butlers or advisers. Now and again there is a picture of him with a woman of interest, like his lover Jean Norton. As he grew older, he wore those large sunhats that made him seem a comic little fellow, half-hidden, with a playful smile. At times the smile seems to be a plea, maybe for understanding or a truce of some kind.

As much as he was part of the great world, he is seldom pictured in groups of people. Usually there are only one or two others, unless he is trying to stump for some cause like Empire Free Trade. This does not imply he was not happy with things. He was an original, oddity, and outcast, all at the same time. An outcast tends to become used to it. Max learned to delight in it. He irritated the mighty and confused the poor, so that both saw him as a peculiarity. As he said of his sons, they would have been much better off going to Harkins Academy, in Newcastle, than to Eton, where three-quarters of his enemies had gone. So, although he took his children to resorts, he must have seen in them the faces of those who were trying to hold him back. And he bullied them because of it.

In certain respects, though, he must have been very lonely. From the time he was twelve, he prosecuted his life from no vantage point but self-will. Lonely? One just has to look over the wreckage of his life, his marriage, and his career.

There is a story of him, one night at a dinner, making fun of many of those titled men who had stabbed him in the back, using quips and barbs they could not answer, in order to entertain a young actress who was sitting beside him. They had titles and no money, he claimed, and they hated his money and begrudged him his title. They were men who, as Peter Howard said, had lost their fortunes, or their fathers' fortunes, and had no ability to make another, so they cursed the man who made his own, and came to them from across the sea (from that land of wolves and primitive Redmen).

The young actress said nothing to him as he used his scathing wit against them. Not for the longest time. Then she turned her pretty little head, and said:

"My dear sir, you are making fun of who you paid to belong to."

He wasn't behaving like a Brit, he was behaving like an American, and they hated him for that too. Or, I should say, to give credit where it is due, he was in a way behaving like a Canadian. It was like the old joke: A Scotsman was asked during the war how he could tell a Brit from an American from a Canadian. The Scot replied that a Brit walked into a bar as if he'd like to own it. An American walked into a bar as if he owned it. A Canadian walked into a bar—he didn't give a fuck who owned it. There was that about Canadians—back then.

CHAPTER SIXTEEN

The Long-Coming Rise of Mr. Bonar Law

Cold, dreary, foggy London in the war. The great monuments are shrouded; there are dirigibles in the sky. It must have been in the back of little Max's mind when he looked out the window of his London hideaway—like a spectre in the fog itself: David Lloyd George's handsome face with its drooping moustache, and his radical posturing. (That was it—the radical posture! As Churchill said of Gandhi, so Max Aitken must have thought of Lloyd George—another con man).

He must have also thought of his good wife, Gladys— perhaps a better wife than people like either Beaver or I deserve—preparing to campaign for him, and then him having to tell her to let it go and step aside, for he had been stabbed in the back by the crème de la crème of British society. No sir, you could never close the drapes on that!

So, after a time, Prime Minister Lloyd George was no longer pleased with our little Max Aitken from far-off Newcastle,

New Brunswick, on the Miramichi. Soon enough Prime Minister David Lloyd George was complaining about him. Complaining about him taking his own view of things, independent of the government. And there was something else. That damned paper, the *Daily Express*, and Max's wish to rupture the cozy alliance between Liberal Lloyd George and Conservative Bonar Law, the one man Lloyd George feared. (He feared Law so much that he often asked Beaver to go to Law's house to break bad news, such as the reinstating of the much-hated Winston Churchill into the wartime cabinet.)

Ah, but wasn't that cozy alliance one that Max helped form?

Aitken stayed at his apartment in grimy old London and waited. And watched. And plotted. Now, he didn't plot directly. No, like a street fighter, he was a spur-of-the-moment kind of guy. A bottle over the head at the right time.

Besides, as much as he wanted to, he couldn't try to bring down this coalition while there was a war.

But the war—as awful as it was, and as long as it did last, and as many empires as it did manage to destroy—did not last for ever. It was over in November 1918, and Max had his papers—and as anyone who ever read anything by him could tell you, one knew when he wrote something, or, even worse, had something written.

As early as August 1918, Max was allowing certain editorials to be printed in the *Express* that would cause the coalition government embarrassment and discomfort.

In one such incident, Lloyd George sent Churchill (now back in cabinet, and Beaverbrook's one remaining Liberal friend) to ask for an explanation about an editorial that was as cutting as it was truthful. The editorial stated that the tottering Liberals were saved from defeat only by the outbreak of world war in 1914 and certain people's (i.e., Lord Beaverbrook's) gracious help. And this in an editorial in a paper owned by a man who was still minister of information for the sitting coalition government.

Beaverbrook would not retract or condemn the editorial, nor would he disclaim credit for it. This is how tough the little bastard was—staring down both Churchill and David Lloyd George at the same time.

As far as Churchill was concerned, as is suggested by Peter Howard and others, this was "a blatant form of political rebellion," and he cautioned Max that he would be sorry to have to deliver this news to the prime minister. Still Max would not draw back. And any Miramicher can understand why. A year and a half before, he had been in a better position in politics than Winston, and had in fact advised him on how to save his career. Now

Churchill was once again in power. No, Max could not draw back!

When the news was delivered, it was reported that Lloyd George decided to let it go. He had enough fights on his hands without taking on Aitken, and he knew he needed the paper's support—or at least its indifference to his political aims. Max knew, in his petulant way, that he had ruffled the feathers of the bird he wanted to bring down. But it would take more than one shot.

MAX AITKEN RESIGNED from office as minister of information in October 1918, due to ill health. Everyone thought he was faking, but he was very ill and, through to the end of the war in November, was in serious jeopardy of losing his life to an abscessed tooth. His resignation, though, also meant that he could turn his full attention to the flaws of a government of which he, up until that time, had been a member.

"Beaverbrook now seemed not merely independent of the Government, but hostile to it, and it was hard to believe that he had once been the intimate friends of Cabinet Ministers," A.J.P. Taylor writes about this period. But men in both parties—those "intimate friends" had dealt him a terrible blow, had kept him on the outside, ridiculed his Empire Free Trade platform and his paper, and for almost ten years had besmirched his name and his far-off Canada. Now they blamed him for having the audacity to fight back.

Max used his paper as a weapon. In fact, why publish a paper that disagreed with your own opinions? No newspaper baron in his right mind would do so. Simply put, he felt an intrusive wartime coalition government was one thing—but a government should not be interfering with an average citizenry after the war, nor should it send more British and Canadian troops in to fight alongside the White Russians in their war against the Bolsheviks. (They were sent.) It was bad for business and bad for everything else, and his was not the only newspaper that wrote this. His was simply the loudest.

There is an aside here: Max and Russia. Max was secretly fascinated with Bolshevism, and even at times applauded it. Perhaps he was not as enthusiastic as Bernard Shaw or other artists (who did not seem to realize that, if they lived in Soviet Russia, they would be the first to disappear), but it seems he did look upon it as a legitimate ideology. He was always hesitant to oppose it. There is, however, the great quip he made in Glasgow, while stumping for Free Trade a few years later. When a Communist shouted him down, saying, "Beaver, have you been to

Russia? There is no unemployment in Russia," Max said, "Yes, I have, and you are right—there is no unemployment in Russia." He paused, and then added, "I've been to the Glasgow jail, and there is no unemployment there either."

I think this was part of his general perversity—to argue any side that rankled those he was arguing with at the time.

Unfortunately for Max, in 1922, just when it seemed that Bonar Law, who had now led the Conservative Party since 1912, might be able to break free of the coalition and lead the Conservative Party to victory, poor health made Law step aside. That left in the running those whom Max distrusted.

Austin Chamberlain, Max's enemy from the party leadership race of 1912, became leader of the Conservative Party within the House of Commons in 1922, and Chamberlain was inclined, as Peter Howard said, to support the coalition. And of course he hated Max Aitken for keeping him from the leadership. But as Max upped his editorial displeasure with the coalition, Chamberlain, in order to embarrass the press baron, suggested that the government was unsuitable to Beaverbrook only because he had businesses and oil interests in the East of which England disapproved. Max had no Eastern oil interests. This was a lie, and one that seriously discredited Max Aitken's motives.

The slander angered Max enough so that, as Peter Howard states, he went to visit Bonar Law. Citing the disrespect he had for Chamberlain, "a yes man" for Lloyd George, he convinced Bonar Law to come out of retirement to be the saviour of the Conservative Party.

Ill and elderly, Bonar Law came back in June 1922 and opposed Chamberlain in a leadership runoff over the very fact of the coalition. The coalition finally fell. In the next general election, the Liberals went down to defeat.

It was a horrendous election. William Manchester writes that Churchill's wife, Clementine, campaigning for her Liberal husband in Ireland, was spit upon. The noble local Irish paper made a point of mentioning that she carried "her un-baptized baby in her arms." Churchill himself was under threat of death, and had armed guards at his door. Beaverbrook of course did not wish this. But he spent money to help the Tory candidates wherever he could. So, in the election of 1922, Bonar Law became what Max had wanted him to be since 1912, prime minister of Great Britain.

Winston's son, Randolph Churchill, stated in his book *Lord Derby, "King of Lancashire"* that "the prime mover and principal agent in the plan to bring down the coalition Government" was Lord Beaverbrook.

Max would become known forever as what Jenkins liked to call, in his biography of Churchill, "a bounder" and a deeply distrusted press baron. And this is much how he is perceived today, even by many in our hometown.

Well, Churchill did not distrust our Max, nor did Bonar Law.

WITH BONAR LAW as prime minister, Max Aitken was perhaps at the height of his power as a back-room strategist. He wanted to use the new power of Bonar Law to support, among other things, his vision of Free Trade. Again, this was the main thing on his mind. Commonwealth Free Trade was to him the balm to keep Britain great, to keep it Imperial, without the need to meddle in Europe, and to safeguard against the great power of the United States, in financial, not military, forums. He wrote about this continually in his papers' editorials.

Max was of his day. He believed in his own supremacy— as a white Englishman. He did not consider that the world had changed and many who had benefited most from Empire no longer claimed they wanted it. Max was old-fashioned and, in his own way, naive—as men from the colonies are at times, who believe in Empire more than those who are more privy to its blessings. In some ways Max believed he was a godsend to the people of England. If not, why would he be there? And it was in some part not only Empire Free Trade but Empire consolidation—a kind of unity, almost like amalgamation—that he was working toward.

But psychologically any talk of Empire after such a terrible war was in bad taste. I don't think Beaverbrook understood this. His time, if he had it (and he did have it), was gone over yonder.

And then, Bonar Law, prime minister for only seven months, died in 1923.

With a vacancy at the top of government, the king had to choose to replace the deceased Bonar Law. It was said the Conservatives wanted to turn toward the common man. So Law's former clerk, and second-term MP, Stanley Baldwin, suddenly found himself "The Man." Truly a quixotic choice.

Prime Minister Stanley Baldwin! From 1923 to 1937 it was to be the age of Conservative leader Stanley Baldwin in Tired Great Britain.

Since they hated each other, it was a stroke of fate that would put Max Aitken into the wilderness for years.

Max was much like Tolstoy's unfortunate dice player. At first, everything he threw worked to his call. From Saint John to London, he could not seem to roll bad dice. Then, after a time, try as he might, the dice no longer went his way.

CHAPTER SEVENTEEN

And Then
Poor Gladys Dies

What kind of life she had, we can imagine. Like one of the characters in *Anna Karenina*, she was left alone with the children for long stretches of time while her husband gallivanted. Some say she did not mind this—the price to pay, so to speak—and was not a great bedfellow for him, often being asleep by nine at night, not really on the same beam. He loved the gay evenings, and sooner or later he kept her from them, simply because of their different needs. Then, after a time, with his politics and finances and other involvements, he lost interest in her and the children. He was an open mark to be blamed for this. He knew and accepted this as well.

She thought of these bed partners of his as trivial encounters. Some say the only love interest she really minded was Jean Norton. A.J.P. Taylor says this was because Norton was someone Beaverbrook wanted to shape and mould and develop, and he could not do this with Lady Beaverbrook, who, as Lord Birkenhead once commented, "had a breeding and a beauty to recommend her to any society in Europe." It was Jean Norton he was in bed with when Gladys came to visit him at his hideaway in London. This is what Beaverbrook's daughter never forgave.

Norton was the wife of a member of parliament, and had children of her own. And she was in Max's league, so to speak; like him she felt a need for companionship at the expense of a more sober spouse. They fought too, Beaver and Jean—but he must have loved her in some way. (Though he said, and I have no reason not to believe him, that the one love of his life was Gladys Drury.) Jean and he travelled together to Europe, played together in Italy, went to Monte Carlo, while her husband—understanding fellow—wanted to help Max with his finances.

Gladys was not so understanding. She decided to fight back. So she told him she was tired of being stuck out in Cherkley and asked to move to London to be closer to him. He relented and bought Stornoway House near Green Park for her. She moved to London with the children, and then found out that the little bugger had moved Jean Norton out to Cherkley. One would have to be callous to even consider this. But it's a gambit that somehow seems naughty rather than harmful. It would, as Miramichers say, have "seemed like a good idea at the time." How much time elapsed after Gladys went out the front door before Jean swooped in the back? Max is not the only one to blame here. What in hell was Jean Norton thinking? Did she think it harmful?

Harmful it was, perhaps in some ways soul-destroying. In 1926, Gladys left for a trip around the world with her daughter Janet. When she came back, Beaver believed he was prepared to settle down with her—to make it all up. She wrote him a letter expressing her love. But she was ill now. He had taken trips all his life with others. Now she went to Belgium alone, hoping for treatment. He wrote her a wonderful letter about how he would change—how she must live. How he would no longer take on the world, how he would spend more time with her. Who knows if he meant it? I know he believed he did.

But he did not get to prove whether he did or not. In fact, he was not to see her again. She came back to Stornoway House and died on December 1, 1927, while he was absent. In fact, Gladys had lived most of her life in Britain alone, far from her family in Canada, and with children who were estranged from a father they hardly knew.

If we want to talk about Max Aitken's tragedy—this was it.

HE DID CHANGE after this in some ways. He never gave up Jean, but now he acquired hiding places, to seek solitude from the world. From here on out he wanted to see no one. From here on out no one could get in touch with him—until he wanted them to. There were new hiding places in England and the Bahamas. In many ways he now hated the world—night life and politics and all of that. But still he needed people near him, so he would call them late at night and ask them over. Late at night—that is the time of the secret extrovert. The comical magician, the game-player. He would arrive in the Bahamas and wire Winston to come and see him.

(This is a real Maritime trait. I can think of a dozen well-known men from the Maritimes who were/are exactly like this. You get a phone call at eleven at night and are asked if you are in the mood for a snack. . . .)

He began to liquidate his assets in Canada and elsewhere. Some say after Gladys died he never went to the *Daily Express* building in London again, except once during the Second World War to show Churchill a movie. This did not mean he released his hold over his paper. No, he wouldn't do that until the 1950s. However, he sold his holdings in cinema and made a fine profit. He also said (rashly) he would take no more interest in the affairs of men. He would go home to Newcastle and live in contemplation. But he never made it back. In fact, after such a time, whatever Newcastle ever was to him was lost.

For whatever reason, he decided to sell his business interests, which allowed him to stay very wealthy during the Depression, when many of his friends sank. Churchill himself came close to bankruptcy then. But Max still kept a keen eye on all his financial affairs. A.J.P. Taylor relates one story about a piano tuner, who was paid for four visits a year and Max thought he had made only three. Max was ready to demand a refund, until he found out the tuner had come the fourth time when he was away.

He gave his affairs in Canada over to his brother Allan, and then bothered him daily. Yet, in these affairs, he made other investors a good deal of money none of them would have made without him. And at times they would be surprised to see huge cheques come to their door. A Mr. Davidson of Newcastle is one example. He wrote to Max complaining that he never had any idea where his money was until a cheque arrived. He was wondering, if the money wasn't forthcoming, would an explanation be?

Whatever he did, he couldn't seem to help it. And though he now hated public affairs, on the public front, some of his greatest battles were just starting.

CHAPTER EIGHTEEN

Free Trade and Stanley Baldwin, I Presume

Initially Beaverbrook and Prime Minister Baldwin were friendly. In his maiden speech to the House of Commons in 1918, he defended and spoke kindly about Max Aitken as minister of information. Perhaps that was the only time he did. Of course, this was a completely political move. He was, in 1918, an unknown wet-behind-the-ears politico, and wanted not to be. Beaver, then being skewered in the House for his propaganda, was the one to champion in a perverse way. Who wouldn't be able to figure that one out? Besides, they had been introduced years before by Baldwin's cousin Rudyard Kipling; and both Aitken and Baldwin revered Bonar Law.

Kipling said that Baldwin was a secret socialist. (He did want the rich to pay down the war debt, and since most of them caused it, I see no real fault in that.) But if Baldwin was a socialist, he was a socialist of comfort. His views assuaged the guilt of privilege. I've always felt that holding views of soft socialism supports the privileged. He had been a history major at Cambridge, and was sensitive about what history would say about him.

He later wondered, for instance, if, given his appeasement attitude of "safety first" in the face of German militarism, from the late twenties right to the brink of the Second World War, history would treat him and Neville Chamberlain unkindly. History has.

The initial rift with Beaverbrook might have come because Baldwin always insisted, and did so publicly, that he was the one who brought Bonar Law back in 1922 and brought Lloyd George down. This did not sit well with Aitken. Baldwin, during his first and second terms, gave half-hearted support to Free Trade, but never enough to commit himself to it. Baldwin hated Max's lax morals. But, as we came to see in his vacillation in the years leading up to the Second World War, there is more than one way to be immoral.

DID AITKEN REALLY KNOW what Free Trade involved, or was it pie in the sky? It seems when he started his campaign in 1929, he had no party support and was rash enough to take on the task, thinking he could single-handedly change the nature of British export. But the problem lay at the top. For Max had no set plan of what he wanted, and not many were patient enough to help him iron it out.

His campaigning stalled, and he took the summer of 1930 off to go sightseeing in Russia. Max had not received the support he felt he deserved from Prime Minister Bennett in Canada, while the support he sought from the government of Stanley Baldwin never came, and Baldwin went down to defeat to Labour, in part because of the animosity of Max Aitken's papers.

Peter Howard reveals that, about this time, Max made a prediction, which was destined to come true—though not as soon as he believed it would; he said that Baldwin, who was very bad for the Conservative Party, would be overthrown. He declared that Churchill, now a Conservative, should lead, but since he wasn't much trusted by anyone, perhaps Neville Chamberlain would take the reins.

"He is as bad as Baldwin," Beaverbrook stated, with some measure of understatement. The truth is that Beaverbrook was very loyal. He backed Churchill almost always—to the annoyance of Clementine. Even when he was angry with the party's direction, Max still supported Churchill as prime minister. This made Winston quip that Beaver, "Loves the rider and dislikes the horse."

BUT IN 1930, the Conservative Party was floundering. Beaverbrook, knowing this, got his meeting with Stanley Baldwin.

What could the Beaver give Baldwin? Well, for one thing, he was the greatest propagandist in the country. Even if he didn't go to the *Express* office, he still ran the paper. If his paper turned its support to the Conservatives again, Baldwin would make much of a speech that Beaver would give on his Free Trade dream to the House of Lords. It wasn't much, but it was all Beaverbrook could ask.

That is, he was always forced to hold the lesser hand now. No one any longer came to him seeking mergers. Government support of a speech in the House of Lords meant nothing. And Beaverbrook's speech in the House of Lords was a failure, for, like many Miramichers, he talked in rough measure with mangled words.

Perversely, he set out in 1930 to independently deliver Free Trade to the Empire. He put in money and mounted his crusade—there is a great picture of him, resembling a somewhat smaller Teddy Roosevelt circa 1912, hat in hand, preaching to the crowd as the wind blew. He stumped and platformed and promised, but it did not come about.

If Free Trade was the one thing in the world that he wanted, he either prepared for it poorly or didn't understand it well enough to sell. Or perhaps the gadget he was trying to sell had been looked over one too many times. For in the end, he was still selling. He was still the salesman walking along the boom road.

MAX'S FAILURE TO DELIVER to Britain and the Commonwealth his vision of Empire Free Trade (flaws and all) in the early 1930s showed the limitations of the Commonwealth itself. It also showed a dying Empire. This uncouth Canadian financier wasn't going to fool Baldwin the way he did those poor Canadians (or, as Baldwin said, the way he was able to fool Bonar Law and Churchill).

For some I have spoken to, Max was a thief because he earned too much money. One has to draw the line—and I've noticed with his greatest detractors that line was/is always drawn with their own intellectual comfort in mind. But the real sore spot with some of these men was that he had earned it not in England, but in the far-off colonies.

Am I defending him? Not a bit of it. I am questioning them. Empire Free Trade failed, and the British Empire was fading to black.

CHAPTER NINETEEN

Signs of a New War

Prime Minister Baldwin was disastrous for Britain and disastrous for Beaverbrook. But Max was in many respects disastrous to himself. And he became more disastrous as time went on. He was a financial genius trying to be a politician, and a brilliant and sometimes revolutionary newspaperman trying to force political policy. He was headstrong and tenacious, and he hated to be outmanoeuvred. It made for many bad days. Once, when he got tired of all his Free Trade battles, he mentioned to Lord Berkinhead that he wished he could go back to those quaint and innocent days when he was plotting to overthrow Lloyd George. But he could not. And much of what he did do after Free Trade seems to be a kind of tarnish. He hung out with lords and ladies, and was instrumental in trying to keep Edward VIII in power, because unlike his friend Churchill, he did not realize the constitutional calamity it would cause. Edward VIII asked for and received the support of Max's paper. (Max was, I am sure, awestruck by the monarchy, and could not say no.)

But Churchill saw it differently. Though he too supported the king and tried to delay the abdication, he believed Edward had a moral and a sacred duty to forget this woman—at least as a wife. Edward of course did not. It all sounds quaint today, and in hindsight, given suggestions about what kind of king Edward would have made, it may have been best for Britain that he did not forget her. But at the time, when love triumphed over duty, it devastated many Britons.

William Manchester relates in *Alone*, the second volume of *The Last Lion*, his three-volume biography of Churchill, that one night, sitting with the Duke of Windsor (formerly Edward VIII) in Monte Carlo, after the coronation of George VI, Churchill told him how he had betrayed the British people, in a way only Churchill could, which did not for one moment lose the tone of respect.

There was a spinelessness about the duke and duchess, who at one point actually believed that a Hitler win would put Edward back on the throne. Many must have hoped for this in the Conservative, Liberal, and Labour parties, judging by the way they ignored Churchill's warnings. And, as writer and broadcaster Alistair Cooke points out, when Paris was about to fall, the duke and duchess were still there, and had to be ordered into the departing car by their chauffeur. "They were at their best," Alistair Cooke said, "when the going was good."

This could never be said about Churchill himself. "There are two Winstons," Max Aitken once said ruefully. "Winston Up and Winston Down. Winston down—with his back to the wall, is magnificent, Winston up—when things are going his way, is intolerable." Both Alistair and Max were right.

AS THE 1930S WORE ON, Max had his games, his dogs—two shitsus that he would carry about and fuss over—his trips with Jean Norton, his paper, his baggage of a past that would not go away. His dreams of going back to Newcastle and living in peace and quiet. He had other lady friends and his games of political intrigue. He was still plotting, still trying to be the boy wonder all over again. When they mention a loose cannon, show a picture of Max in a sunhat, smiling out from under its brim.

The men of power he kept tabs on were the ones, almost to a man, who he felt had forced him into the House of Lords in 1917, which meant that Max's cannon was always firing in every direction. But he could never fire fast enough or get them all—and even to his adversaries he could and would be surprisingly generous. He once gave Baldwin, who had hurt him more than any other politician save Lloyd George, £25,000, telling him to give it to the charity of his choice. Baldwin said the reason for this was an accident in which Max came close to death, and he was afraid. Well maybe—but I guarantee it was never Baldwin he feared.

He learned of Hitler's rise to power, and watched, numbed, as his Conservative Party turned on the only man in the country who might be able to defend them: Winston Churchill. During these years, Churchill almost lost his seat, certainly lost his cabinet seat, and needed spies within caucus just to find out what was going on. He was laughed at by people like Bernard Shaw. (Well, who wasn't? Shaw was good at laughing, often at better men.)

But Neville Chamberlain and Stanley Baldwin were determined to prove Churchill wrong, and they prostrated themselves to one of the most evil men in history in order to do so. As Hitler said about these men in 1944: "My enemies are worms—I met them in Munich."

When future prime minister Clement Attlee said that Beaverbrook was one of the most evil men he had ever met, he was at the same time agreeing on policy with those who smirked at Churchill and dined with German Foreign Minister Ribbentrop (later hanged for war crimes).

But then again, most people seemed to lack foresight in those times. "Scholarships not battleships!" was a chant that was used against Churchill and his ilk.

"Insensible," said Sir Archibald Sinclair, then head of the Liberal Party, when asked about the prospects of a British continental army. This was in 1938.

But Beaver did not want war either—and said as much. "No War This Year" his paper stated in 1939. And he too had friends both Italian and German.

That is, he vacillated just as others did. He went to clubs, and ate with pacifists, as well as anyone else. There were leftists on his paper now, like Michael Foot, who later became a Labour minister and was a long-time friend. Still, for most of this time, Beaverbrook was the only support Churchill had.

He allowed Churchill to publish his so-called "war mongering" in the *Daily Express* when no one else in the land would give him a platform and Winston gave his speeches to an empty House of Commons. "You were given a choice between war and dishonour, you chose dishonour and you will have war!"

(Though even Max refused to publish Winston for a stretch in 1938—as a favour to appeaser Neville Chamberlain, then the prime minister.)

On another front, Aitken brought former Canadian prime minister R.B. Bennett, who had betrayed him on Empire Free Trade, to Britain and got him a knighthood, and taught him what wines to serve with dinner. Max had a father figure beside him again, and he seemed to enjoy his company.

During this time there were moments when Max had an uncanny ability to see with a clarity few men had.

An editorial in his *Evening Standard* sounded a warning about the enthusiasm over the Munich Pact—while, like most papers, supporting it.

It is also interesting to note that one of the great men of the century, George Orwell, criticized Beaverbrook's papers for pacifism in the face of danger. Still, it might have been wiser for Orwell to understand that the left-wing papers he himself had at one time cherished called for peace right up until Hitler invaded Russia in 1941.

Max did not like the guarantee given to Poland by the British government—that if it was attacked by Germany, England would respond—because the guarantee was given without consulting the Dominions.

He also disagreed with the mutual-defence pact with France, sensing that, if push came to shove, France would capitulate, and Britain would be on its own defending Poland, which could not defend itself. Strategically he was right—as it turned out, deadly right.

He was wrong, however, from the standpoint of moral obligation, and he was wrong to keep Churchill off his pages, however briefly. When Baldwin kept Churchill out of his third cabinet, for fear he would anger Hitler, Winston boldly said that no greater crime had been committed since Roman emperor Caligula appointed his horse a senator. He was laughed at; he was right.

But no matter what people wanted, war came in 1939. And as it would turn out, without Beaverbrook the Battle of Britain might well have been lost and England's neck wrung like a chicken.

As Churchill famously said during a speech to the Canadian parliament: "Some chicken, some neck."

Beaverbrook provided much of the early gristle in that tough neck.

CHAPTER TWENTY

War and the Boy from Newcastle

The war came in September 1939, spellbinding in its seeming stupidity. Hitler, self-mesmerized, had no choice. No one was around to stop him. And perhaps that grandest puppet master of all, Soviet leader Joseph Stalin, was egging him on. (Some biographers actually say this, and believe that Stalin was expecting an attack. Whether or not this was so, he made the most of it in the end.) Hitler, too, thought Britain's promise to Poland was an ill-considered one, and they wouldn't hold to it. He was wrong. Prime Minister Chamberlain had a moral obligation to Poland, and tried his best to prosecute the war, and then resigned. Grudgingly, he handed over the reins to Churchill. And Churchill's war cabinet appointed Max Aitken as minister of aircraft production.

He was now an unwilling player, with his asthma and ill health, yet here he would be an almost indispensable one. Within a few months he more then quadrupled the manufacture of aircraft. Each day he was slandered in the House of Commons for duplicity and mismanagement, and he kept going. When the Continental army was forced from Dunkirk in May 1940, he made every effort to retrieve spare airplane parts that were left behind.

There is a story, related by Peter Howard in his book *Max the Unknown*, of Aitken going to see Churchill and meeting in the foyer a high-ranking naval commander who delightedly told him that a new shipment of steel for his destroyers had arrived. Max said great, and, pulling rank, went in to see Churchill first.

"What's happening, Max?" Winston asked.

"I just got a great shipment of steel for our planes," Max said.

"Wonderful news," Winston beamed.

He was the boy giving his landlady her fifty cents all over again.

There are those who said he did not do what he said he was going to do, and that he fudged the results. Historian Roy Jenkins seems to think this, or at least intimates that Max was not that important. As with almost all of what Jenkins says about Beaverbrook, I am going to disagree.

It is widely suggested that, when he took over as minister of aircraft production, there were five Spitfires in reserve—

that is, once the pilots were in the air, five aircraft were left in the hangars.

Four months later, 6,400 aircraft had been built. Where did Aitken get most of the raw materials? From Canada and the States. Where did he get many of the pilots? From Canada as well. He bartered to get machinery and engines from Detroit. When Henry Ford said he would not build engines for belligerents in a war that did not concern the United States, Max used his old connections with Rolls-Royce to get engines and went to the smaller Packard Motor Car Company to build them. Some say that, because of this, he had a hand in jump-starting American production for its own war effort. He spoke of thousands and thousands of planes. Did he fudge the records? Probably—he was Beaverbrook. Did he come up against a bureaucratic wall? Of course, this was England. Was he fighting for England's life? Absolutely. His arguments would start in cabinet, against one, and then two, and then sooner or later he would be taking on all comers, with poor Churchill trying to keep the peace daily.

"He swept through every department like Genghis Khan—it was remarkable," said Air Force colonel Moore-Barbazon, member of parliament for Chatham. "He was one of the people Churchill spoke about when he said, 'Never was so much owed by so many to so few!'" (This is not a well-known summation of that famous line.)Was he indispensable? For a little while, a little while as indispensable as Eisenhower or Marshal Zhukov. Did he make enemies? Of course he did, he was . . .

No one was going to mess with Max Aitken. He was the inspired little tough from the town of Newcastle, on the banks of the Miramichi. If he had been intimidated by anyone, he wouldn't have made it out of Newcastle. That's the secret that Small Town boys know.

But he kept going. Not only with his aircraft production, but with his intrigues and his papers. In fact, he knew exactly what was being said against the present administration in his papers, and didn't always do anything to stop it, although he was portrayed as the puppet master of his employees. Churchill and others complained in 1940 of leftists in his employ. The Beaver responded that there may well be, but that didn't mean he agreed with them. He also complained that he was accosted on both sides: on one for telling his employees what to say, and on the other for not telling them what to say.

During this time certain of his younger friends, including journalist Peter Howard, wrote the pamphlet *The Guilty Men*, attacking Chamberlain, Baldwin, Lord Halifax, and the rest for the terrible lack of British preparedness. Certainly Beaver approved of this pamphlet. So would most of us. He yelled for metal, tin, and copper—he had people give anything they could to be melted down and used to make his planes. He demanded the gates from former prime minister Baldwin's estate, and said he would send the police to take them. He must have delighted in this, but he was outvoted in parliament, and Baldwin's iron gates stayed. (However, Max's gates and railings at Stornoway House were taken with Max's blessing.)

CERTAIN NOTES FROM 1940 show what a man of mettle he actually was. Bombers were being built in the United States, pushed across the border to Canada, flown to Halifax, Nova Scotia, and put on ships to England. Those that weren't sunk by the U-boat packs had to be reassembled at their destination. This to Beaverbrook was a criminal waste of time. He proposed to Churchill and got the go-ahead to hire Canadian, American, and Australian bush pilots to fly these planes across the Atlantic, and he then requisitioned and built an airport in Gander, Newfoundland, to get it done. Members of the British High Command howled at his presumption. Of course. Max went ahead. Of course. This was simply the bravest policy decision concerning aircraft in the Second World War.

He also sought and got a dispersal of aircraft-production centres, to thwart the enemy and lessen its bombing successes, but was unsuccessful in trying to stop air-raid sirens, because, he maintained, they slowed work production.

When his son-in-law, Drogo Montagu, Janet's second husband (a fighter pilot and son of the Earl of Sandwich), was killed in the Battle of Britain, Max phoned his friend Peter Howard to say that nothing but total victory would ever ensure peace. And he sounded genuinely heartbroken.

He was to break Churchill's heart too. As Peter Howard records, when First Sea Lord Dudley suggested the French fleet be destroyed to save it from falling into German hands, Churchill was aghast, and asked Max for his opinion on the matter.

"Attack it immediately," Aitken replied. "The Germans will force the French fleet to side with the Italians in the Mediterranean Sea! They will do it by blackmail. They will threaten to burn Marseilles, or even to burn Paris, if the French do not comply." For someone who hadn't wanted war, he certainly understood what had to be done once the game was on. Max later recounted what followed. Churchill gave the order; Churchill wept.

There was another moment recorded by both A.J.P. Taylor and Peter Howard. It came when certain naval officers were considering sending the British fleet to Canada if there was an invasion on British soil. Churchill, after receiving this note from the Naval office, handed it to Aitken. It was Canada they were thinking of sending the fleet to, and Aitken should be informed. But Aitken knew this would look like capitulation to the Americans, whose support they badly needed. Max simply said: "Winston, you can't do that," and it was settled.

Though Beaverbrook distrusted the Americans, he realized they were desperately needed, and he would be the man sent to barter with them.

"I've come to ask for your help, and I'm going to ask for a lot," he quipped to the U.S. Senate.

THERE WERE OF COURSE other things not so settled. One was Beaver himself. His unfortunate perversity of temperament, his anger at slights, that stayed with him most of his life, threatened to derail him and the part he played in the war effort. This was his finest hour, but he had to be prodded into staying on duty. It was unconscionable to request retirement so often, even more than Sea Lord Fisher in 1915, and it doesn't sit well in retrospect. If it is aggravating now to have to read, imagine what it was like for Winston Churchill, who thought Beaverbrook his ablest minister.

"I am placing my entire confidence, and to a large extent the life of the state upon your shoulders," Churchill wrote to a disgruntled Max in January 1941.

But Max had legitimate concerns. He was awake day and night, was blasted in the House for everything he tried to do, and was not well. And, as always, he was considered an intriguer. Also, he was frightened of the bombs that were dropping. He made no bones about his fear, and so more power to him that he stayed, and remained the most insistent force—except of course for Churchill himself—in wartime Britain. But just as when he was a boy of twelve, he wanted and needed to be his own man, and with Winston as both prime minister and minister of defence, it was hard to be that. Nonetheless, as Churchill wrote of Beaverbrook years later: "He did not fail—this was his hour." Of course, as Max knew, this was also Winston's hour. It was his finest hour, and the finest hour of the British people. The only other people at that time to show so much courage were the Russians. But that was to come.

Max here—as usual—is not above criticism. The unfortunate fact is that he never was. That Churchill had to take time out of his busy office to deny his requests for resignation and write countless letters saying his resignation was not accepted, and to try and cajole him into staying, is nothing short of ingratitude on Max's part. Any disappointment or contradiction of his orders encouraged him to vent his anger and browbeat Churchill, who had too much to worry about already. One has to feel for Churchill here, who was waging a war for the very survival of his country—while certain other countries in Europe gleefully hid up Hitler's arse.

Max's relationships with other men of power would always be a double-edged sword, and as he built his planes, he pressed Churchill far too much. Finally, Churchill made Max overall minister of production.

There was an uproar, on a huge scale. Ernest Bevin, a rising star in the Labour Party, and Attlee, who would become Labour prime minister, were firmly against him, and Max, who for a short time had been a hero with Labour because of his fall 1941 visit to Soviet Russia, where he had signed a pact to send large-scale supplies to their war effort, was now losing influence.

As the crisis surrounding Beaverbrook grew, all during the dark December of 1941 Churchill was facing his own political disasters. Singapore fell to the Japanese. After Pearl Harbor on December 6, the Americans, who had promised much material support, were in need of most of it themselves. Rommel was playing havoc with the British in the

North African desert, and the public no longer trusted Churchill as both prime minister and minister of defence. Winston was working twenty-hour days. Sooner or later, if Attlee and others wanted Max gone, and if Max continued to insist on having his own way—as he had from the time he was a schoolboy—Churchill, already fighting rear-guard actions to protect himself, would no longer be able to protect Aitken.

In February 1942, Max defined his authority as minister of production. It would in essence put everything, including shipbuilding, under his control. He would be his own man with everything concerning war production, or no man at all. This was always his way, from the moment he stepped on the train and met Mr. Stairs and tried to sell him a typewriter.

But he was playing with fire here. For Churchill knew that, once gone, Max would this time (for all intents and purposes) be gone for good.

IN THE WINTER OF 1942, after parrying with Aitken for a year or more and now in deep political trouble himself, Churchill felt he had to reshuffle his cabinet. Peter Howard and others state that Winston showed Max two lists. On one, Max was in the cabinet, and on the other, Max was out.

Max, looking over the lists, became miffed, and said he wanted out, especially if Attlee was to be deputy prime minister. Churchill felt he had to have Attlee.

Then, in deference to Attlee, Winston chose Stafford Cripps rather than Beaverbrook as leader of the House of Commons.

Preferring Cripps—or anyone else in the realm—was to Max a slap in the face, and a betrayal from an old friend, perhaps the best friend in England he had ever had. More stinging was this: Stafford Cripps had attacked Max's plans to help the Soviet Union—for, of all things, being too generous. This was one of the achievements of which Max was most proud—having gone to Russia in the depths of the war and signed a pact with Molotov, even having redirected some of England's own materials from Canada and the United States to help Moscow fight the war. (Because of this, Max would be awarded the Soviets' Order of Sovorov in 1944.)

Max told Winston that he would not serve in a government with Attlee as deputy prime minister. Attlee had done nothing to deserve this plum, he argued. It has been stated that, at this point, Churchill became exasperated, and told him to repeat his threat of resignation in front of Attlee and Cripps themselves. Max, in his usual huff, took the dare and did just that. Once he had done so, Churchill could no longer pretend he had not, and was forced to accept his resignation. Cripps and Attlee were ecstatic over this, and Churchill was deeply sorry.

Here was the man who had built the Spitfire (with the help of Canada, and among others K.C. Irving and the woods of New Brunswick), which won the battle over the skies of Britain; the man who had ordered and financed the building of the Gander runway, so that bomber planes he had parlayed and fought for could take off and fly the treacherous North Atlantic. Here was the man who had gone to Australian, Canadian, and American bush pilots, some of them women, to get the job done. And all the while he was laughed at and ridiculed for doing so by men who would sleep safer and quieter because he had not relented in his job.

Max believed Churchill had betrayed him. But the war was the most important thing, and victory the most important aim, and Churchill, sinking in the polls at that time, could only be so loyal. (Winston had to face a vote of no confidence later, in July of 1942. This is how he was rewarded by the House of Commons.) Max Aitken in a year and a half had done far more for England than Attlee or Cripps or anyone else in the wartime government, except for Winston himself, would ever do.

When a boy, Max was very good at Birds in a Bush—a game in which one guesses the number of marbles in another boy's hand. He was so good at it that it seemed almost diabolical. He had also played dice with lumber barons on the Miramichi when he was sixteen. He was always good at games of chance.

He could never sit still. As a child he had listened to his father's sermons, not at his mother's side but up in the church balcony, as far away as he could get, fidgeting and wanting to be somewhere else. This eccentric had learned all his disobedience and human insight as a boy of seven—and had relied upon it to help save the Western world. He was now undercut by those who had always listened to sermons and would never wager anything on a game of Birds in a Bush. In a very grave way, those who couldn't count the number of hairs on the teacher's moustache, those who had sat in school, and raised their hands, and studied hard had taken their revenge, and congratulated each other that they had done so, while a bewildered Churchill, who cared for him more than he did ten of any others, could do nothing to help.

The Beaver went away to a flat on the first floor of the *Evening Standard* building.

This was because Stornoway, Gladys's beloved house, had been bombed in the autumn of 1940.

CHAPTER TWENTY-ONE

Comrade Stalin's Man

A player of that talent doesn't sit things out. So Max was sent as an envoy to Washington, and although what future British prime minister Harold Macmillan said at the time was true— that Max was suffering from twenty-hour days, months of strain and work, and was exhausted—he kept up a busy schedule. He seemed to convince—or share the opinion with—Roosevelt (they had New Brunswick in common; Max from the Miramichi, Roosevelt on Campobello) that a second front was necessary in 1942 to relieve Stalin's army.

To Beaverbrook this was a new cause, and a way to stick it to those who had pushed him aside in Britain. Besides, for him, the success of another front was simply a matter of logistics: cut out the unnecessary campaigns in North Africa, and get down to business attacking the Germans in France.

It would prove far more difficult than it seemed. (Even by the time D-Day rolled around in June 1944, the Germans were still a massive and formidable force and came close on a number of occasions to turning the Allied advance.)

It would also mean a strategic shifting of the whole war effort. It really does show Max at his worst. Field Marshal Erwin Rommel would then have had a one-way ticket to the oilfields of Russia—with his Afrika Corps freed from their duties in North Africa. In fact, Rommel always planned to do this, if he could defeat General Bernard Montgomery's Eighth Army.

As Peter Howard says, the Allies also would have had to stop aircraft production to start wholesale landing-craft production. Churchill did not want to hear about it, and did not want Max sent back to Britain as Roosevelt's quasi-representative. This showed Max as Max, a political gadfly—who now suddenly wanted to please his new friend, Joseph Stalin, and prove to his old enemies in the House of Commons that he was still the main talent, the boy wonder after all these years. More subtly, he also wanted to take Roosevelt's immense power and use it to browbeat his enemies in London as well.

So hear, hear! Friends with Roosevelt, after a life of distrusting the Americans. And friends with Uncle Joe, too! Yes, that same Joseph Stalin who murdered twenty-six million of his own people.

Stalin had earlier influenced envoys Max (for the British) and Averell Harriman (for the United States) when they visited Moscow in 1941 by saying that the paucity of their offers meant that the West was happy Germany had attacked Russia and wanted Russia to fail. There was no "paucity"— Max saw to it. But Stalin was not completely wrong, as John Lukacs states in his book of essays on Churchill, *Churchill: Visionary, Statesman, Historian*. Stalin might have been right to think Churchill wanted Hitler to attack Russia, but he was wrong to think Churchill wanted Stalin to lose.

Now Stalin, with his country fighting on a wide front from Leningrad near the Finnish border, through Moscow, southeast to Stalingrad, needed relief. A second front was to him essential.

How did Max convince himself that he liked Stalin? Well, Stalin was a rogue and a drinker. And Max liked all rogues and drinkers. Besides, Stalin could make himself likeable! And he had fooled more than Max. He had fooled Roosevelt, and to a degree Churchill. But as for Max and Stalin? Both came from religious backgrounds. Both hated the aristocracy and the pomposity of so-called experts. Max did not see Koba (Stalin's nickname) as a mass murderer greater than Hitler. (This showed another terrible blind spot, and perhaps a Miramichi one: the belief that rogues are more drinkers than destroyers. Perhaps this appealed, in a foolhardy way, to Max's own personal vanity, as rogue extraordinaire.) He took up Stalin's cause—just as he had done all of his life with others—and suddenly became the loudest voice for a second front.

So he went about explaining Comrade Stalin to the American press, with opinions that were partially true. Here is what Max Aitken said to support Mr. Stalin. It really shows him to be, on this occasion, most foolhardy.

He said that there was no religious persecution in Soviet Russia. He was right as far as the war years went. Stalin knew he had to open the churches for his population to bear down and fight, and religious persecution was halted (or abated) for the first time in twenty years. People were allowed to pray in front of icons—some were icons of people Stalin himself had butchered—and take communion. Religious persecution would start in earnest again after the war. Max said there was no persecution of the Jews, and he was right, as far as it went. Stalin started his campaign against the Jews after Golda Meir visited in 1948, when he began to worry that his Jewish population had only one capital, Jerusalem. Max also said Russia had the most heroic soldiers and greatest generals. Well, no more heroic than the British, American, Australian, or Canadian (or German or Japanese, for that matter), but fighting on their own ground. Certainly they had the greatest general in Marshal Zhukov (who was demoted as soon as the war was over). Besides this, when drinking and singing folk songs, Stalin was roguish and fun. That was the only side of Stalin that Max Aitken wanted to see.

Max did not understand (and would go to his death without understanding) that this time the father figure he had chosen was most deadly—a man who was a God in his own country, a man who, along with Hitler, could be said to symbolically be represented by the two combatants Milton spoke about in *Paradise Lost*: "So frowned the Mighty Combatants that hell grew darker with their frowns/ So matched they stood."

Churchill, embarrassed and disappointed in Max, wanted to silence him, and asked if he would like to be British ambassador in Washington—that is, a man who must follow the party line. Beaver was to remain in Washington and replace Lord Halifax. Halifax agreed to this. Roosevelt agreed. Churchill agreed. Then Max declined— unless there was a second front.

This act of disrespect smacks of wilful immaturity after sixty years.

So, there was no ambassadorship. But Max kept insisting, spoke to the New York papers about how a second front was needed . . .

WE ALL KNOW Max Aitken got his wish. A quasi–second front came in August 1942. But it was done in a way that was almost calculated to prove to him that he was mistaken—and to prove to his last great mentor, Joe Stalin, that such a thing was just not feasible at the time. It was a deadly frontal assault on a beach at Dieppe, by Canadian soldiers running up beaches against heavily armed pillboxes and impenetrable defensive positions, and Max bore the responsibility and felt the sting. At least in some way, because those who were against it wanted him to. Was this conscious or unconscious slaughter to prove a point to the boy from Newcastle? Who knows? Perhaps in the god-awful fog of war, both. Max did not see it coming until it was too late. For years after, he blamed Louis Mountbatten, the overlord of the operation, for the Canadian casualties at Dieppe.

"Shake the hand of a Canadian you haven't killed," Max said when he met Mountbatten soon after.

It was a fiasco, without any air or naval support (which the Canadians right up until the moment of the battle were promised). It was a humiliation in which his Canadians fought and died—and not only this, but some made it, through withering hellfire to the town of Dieppe itself, an almost impossible feat of heroics. Max, shaken to the core, gave up his second-front campaign. For the rest of the war he spoke of other things to which the government should be committed—the price of commodities, etc., and pretty much left the decisions of the war to Churchill.

After this, he joined cabinet meetings only as an adviser, and in 1943 he took up agriculture and farming to help the war effort. He wasn't a great farmer himself, of course, but as always he made sure those he hired or consulted were. He even sent honey to Attlee's wife, and it has been said that the Attlees appreciated it. (So perhaps he wasn't so evil after all.)

Late in the war, in 1945, as he was sitting in a war cabinet meeting, a note was handed to him simply stating: "Jean is dying."

Churchill, seeing the note, announced: "The cabinet can do no more business today."

A.J.P. Taylor states that Jean Norton's death was Max's greatest loss since Gladys in 1927. He might marry again, late in life, but the two great loves of that life were gone.

CHAPTER TWENTY-TWO

Last Years

In the end he was, in a way, far more British than the British, in a way more Imperial than any, more certain that things had to be done in a certain way. Of course he was always like this. It was his way or the highway. Still and all, he was the consummate outsider in a world that pretended (and only pretended) to like outsiders.

The portrait of him painted by Graham Sutherland in 1953, which hangs in the foyer of the Beaverbrook Art Gallery in Fredericton, New Brunswick, shows an elderly imp, with that smile that always displayed a hint of cunning mischief. As one biographer said, he was still the Prince of Mischief. Mischief was his great asset and liability. That and the ability to be at times four moves ahead of everyone else.

After the war, the country was going in another direction. He found himself quite suddenly an old man, all his dreams now out of fashion with the times.

He was seen in Chatham, near his old law office one day by a group of North Shore Regiment soldiers. My wife's uncle Bill Savage, wounded at D-Day as a boy of seventeen, was one. They hollered at him:

"Beaver—thanks for getting staples to us in the war."

And one said:

"Well the war is over. What about some of that money now?"

He laughed heartily at this and, putting his hands in his pockets, turned them inside out, to show he hadn't a cent on him. Then they all laughed at that. He was the boy of eight again, playing Birds in a Bush.

He got the name Beaverbrook put up on Tweedie's lawfirm's office door. But he didn't stay. He had nowhere left to go. He went back to England.

He was an elderly man now, wearing straw hats in sunny places, attendants at his side, smiling wanly at the camera. He resigned from the Conservative Party in 1949. His dreams of Imperial preference gone, he chained the lady at the top of his newspaper masthead. He hadn't given up the fight for it until 1952. By then, he and Churchill knew that the world of Britain was fading, that it was America's world now. Churchill sat in the House, and became prime minister once more, but Beaverbrook was gone from active politics. He did seem in the end to have the grace to know when to leave. His best days were behind him by thirty-five years. By the mid 1950s he knew this, and seemed contented.

The old world had crumbled beneath him, just as it had done an age before to the Victorians. For some reason, pictures of him as an old man seem to me to be most significant. In one, he stands silently to the side while Senator John F. Kennedy speaks with the president of the University of New Brunswick, Colin B. Mackay. He had known old Joe, Kennedy's father, who was an Irish-American and hadn't wanted America supporting Britain in the war. All of that was over now.

The old war horse spoke of the new power-brokers with amusement and not without a hint of sarcasm—of the new prime ministers with disdain. They would have been no match for him, just as Churchill said about himself with the same people. But they were old men going on their final journey on unsteady feet. There is a picture of Max and Winston with Harold Macmillan, taken in 1962. They are sitting together on a couch, and we sense that each of them is attended by aides. In formal evening attire, they face the camera without looking at it, and seem to acknowledge each other without even a glance. Only people who have come through wars together can do so.

"I met an old man who couldn't piss. I can piss, I just can't walk," the Beaver once said.

Once, when Churchill did not remember a gift Max had sent him, he said: "My friends are going from the head down. I am going from the feet up." He was.

He was still writing books. He wrote a biography of Lloyd George, and had one planned on his arch-enemy Baldwin that he did not write, or at any rate did not complete. His books have a style that is pure . . . Beaverado. You can see it in everything he wrote. He had to be king-maker and king-breaker. And if you love him, then you accept that. Beyond this, in his words there is a slight indication that he was never really sure exactly why things happened. But he knew they did. He also tried to get his life in order, and began a campaign to give many of his assets away.

He was still railed at and belittled by people. One of these was the once-famous British journalist and philosopher Malcolm Muggeridge—a man incensed that Beaverbrook should have money and power. What is even more telling about Muggeridge (and this is the real bone of contention he raises) how dare he spread his largesse to lowly backward New Brunswickers? You see, that was the thinking when Muggeridge said that there were more statues to Beaverbrook in New Brunswick than there were churches. (Muggeridge lied of course.) Yet Muggeridge persisted without saying what rankled him: What rankled

Malcolm was a man giving so much to so many supposedly illiterate people from the winter dark.

Well, I came from that winter dark, that backward province too. I grew up two blocks from Max's old home, roamed the same streets at night. I took in the same offices of adventure, and displeased the same kinds of people, and made my way in a world that was as often as closed toward me as his was toward him.

Max seemed to know that. He seemed to know that Christ, wherever he might be in the hearts of men, would embrace a boy from Harkins every bit as warmly as a boy from Harrow. But there are always people who just never catch on.

MAX'S HEALTH FLUCTUATED and so did his interests. He took trips to France, and planned books that he did not start or did not finish.

He gave the Beaverbrook Art Gallery to New Brunswick in 1958—filled with paintings by Salvador Dali, Gainsborough, Sir Josiah Reynolds, Sutherland, Picasso, Matisse, and many others. Great New Brunswick artists like Millar Britain and Jack Humphrey were represented there too. (As was my uncle Harry Richards in 1965.) Though, as I write this, ownership of the collection is being contested by his grandchildren, who for some reason, say they are "hurt" by the people of New Brunswick, whom they "care for." Let's just say they have captured the spirit and essence of those British their grandfather fought so valiantly against.

The Old Manse Library where I first wrote is now the Beaverbrook Museum. Many other buildings besides these bear his name.

He did not do this so much for himself—and why should it matter if he did? He gave because it made him feel good, and perhaps important. So what? He donated money and became a chancellor of the University of New Brunswick. He never asked for a penny back.

He retired to his great estate at Cherkley. He took trips to France, kept up with his old papers: "What's the news?" he would say whenever he answered the telephone.

He still loved and bought the newest gadgets, just like the typewriter he had carried on the train all those years before.

Once in France, at a party, the Duke of Windsor was showing off a pair of expensive cufflinks that the duchess had bought for him. Everyone began to show their own, except for Max. Finally cajoled into it, he drew back his jacket sleeves to reveal safety pins in his shirt, just like those he had worn to the dance in Saint John when he was eighteen. He had never escaped his youth after all.

He married again late in life. The new Lady Beaverbrook was Lady Christofor Dunn, the widow of Sir James Dunn, the financier he had met in Edmonton when he was nineteen years of age.

In the 1950s he received honorary doctorates from Mount Allison and Saint Thomas universities. The tribute speeches written for these investitures by the universities were gushing and almost embarrassing proclamations of our province's reverence for him.

We used to see him about town also. I admit the dates are vague, but my father pointed him out to me one day, in 1958 or 1959. All I saw was a little stooped elderly man getting into a car in front of the town hall. I was too far away to say hello, and probably would have been too tongue-tied if I had been closer.

He used to stop youngsters on the road, asking them if they would like to go for a drive. He took my friend Don Doiron for pop and chips in his car, when he was in Beaverbrook Settlement one day. Don told me he was amazed that a man would sit in the back seat and have a driver. That self-pleasing innocence would all be looked upon as strangely suggestive today, wouldn't it? Don sat beside him in ratty sneakers and shorts, and Max spoke to Don about fishing trout in the brook nearby, just as he had done long ago. He pointed out to his driver old men and women whom he said he knew. He probably did. Another boy he invited for a ride said he couldn't go because he had a baseball game. I once told this to an American professor who dissolved in cackling laughter at the boy's answer. It is not the boy's fault. He was just a boy going to a baseball game. Still, the boy remembered the incident. Most likely the game and who won is long forgotten.

Why did Beaver do this? Was he looking for his lost youth? Did he wish to revitalize himself? Or was he trying to make sure others remembered him? All of this and more, of course! He was, after all is said and done, trying to remember the way it should have been for him—and trying to instill what he thought the memories should be into the hearts and souls of others. This is really the greatest contest he had. But he couldn't do it. He would fail at this as well—and though he had done more than most men ever would, I am sure he often thought of himself as a failure. For it is impossible for a man who had that much ambition to ever succeed. As much as Max championed himself, as much as he bragged—and he did brag always—part of him felt he had failed. He kept coming home so people could tell him he hadn't. That was a trick, too. But in the end, he couldn't convince himself that he was home, so he went back to his adopted nation.

THE CANADIAN PRESS BARON Lord Thomson gave him a tribute dinner in London when he was turning eighty-five, and flew four New Brunswick First Nation chiefs, two Micmac and two Maliseet, over as a surprise for the celebration. One Micmac chief, Mosey Francis, of Eel Ground, a reserve near Newcastle, brought back a piece of birthday cake. His granddaughter Hazel has told me it is still in their possession.

A British newspaper interviewed Max, and found him to be an "echoing gallery through which stump all the great figures of half a century." The interviewer asked him the one question: Was he sorry about not being able to accomplish Free Trade.

"I was unworthy," he said quietly.

In his final speech, he told those gathered that he had been an apprentice all his life, from those first days back in Chatham, and that he would soon depart for somewhere else—he was not sure of the direction—but he would be an apprentice once more. He returned to Cherkley and was not seen again.

He died on June 9, 1964, in the arms of his wife Christofor. There was a service at Saint Paul's Cathedral. Then, in September, on a warm fall afternoon, just the kind he himself would have skipped school for, his ashes were brought back to Newcastle and placed in his bust, which stands in the town square. Led by our teachers, we all went in double file from school to the park, me and my brothers and sisters, and my wife, Peg, though I did not know her then. There was a tribute, the bugle sounded, and a gun salute rang out under the clear blue sky. Some of the buildings he knew as a boy, now tottering in old age, surrounded him.

My wife's cousin, a cadet named David Savage, handed the Canadian flag to Max's widow. There was much dignity and solemnity in honour of a man many of us could not remember. In some way the Miramichi was his Rosebud. Like Citizen Kane, he loved it dearly and missed it always; but perhaps he had forgotten along the way where he laid it down. That didn't seem to matter any more. For this was his river, and the wanderer was now, at long last, back home.

1879	William Maxwell Aitken is born in Maple, Ontario, on May 25.
1880	The Aitken family moves to Newcastle, New Brunswick.
1892	The first of Max's newspapers is published.
1896	Aitken meets Mr. Tweedie and goes to work at his law firm; meets R.B. Bennett and James Dunn; and runs Bennett's first campaign.
1897	Max enrols in Saint John Law School, but doesn't complete studies.
1898	Aitken follows Bennett to Alberta.
1899–1900	Max sells bonds door-to-door.
1902	John Fitzwilliam Stairs founds Royal Securities Corp. and hires Aitken.
1904	Stairs dies and Max Aitken becomes general manager of Royal Securities Corp.
1906	Gladys Drury and Max Aitken are married.
1907	Max moves to Montreal and acquires a seat on the stock exchange.

1908   Janet Gladys Aitken, Max's first child,
            is born.

1910   Aitken becomes embroiled in Canada
            Cement scandal, moves to London, and wins
            seat for Unionist (Conservative) Party in
            Ashton-under-Lyne. Max's second child,
            John William Maxwell Aitken, is born.

1911   Max Aitken is knighted. Bonar Law becomes
            leader of the Opposition.

1912   Peter Rudyard Aitken, Max's third child, is born.

1914   At the outbreak of the First World War, Aitken
            becomes Canada's "eye-witness" at the Front.

1915   Aitken becomes a representative of the
            Canadian government with the Canadian
            Expeditionary Force and creates the Canadian
            War Records Office.

1916   Max writes *Canada in Flanders*; buys the
            controlling interest in the *Daily Express*; and
            is made a baronet. David Lloyd George
            becomes British prime minister.

1917   Aitken is raised to the peerage and takes the
            title Lord Beaverbrook.

1918	In February, Aitken joins the British cabinet and is made minister of information in charge of propaganda; in October, he resigns from office.
1920s	Aitken builds a chain of newspapers, including the *Daily Express*, the *Evening Standard*, and the *Sunday Express*.
1922	Bonar Law becomes prime minister of Britain.
1923	Bonar Law dies; Stanley Baldwin becomes prime minister.
1927	In December, Max's wife, Gladys, dies.
1929	Beaverbrook champions the Empire Free Trade movement (and through the 1930s).
1936	Max tries to keep Edward VIII in power.
1937	Neville Chamberlain becomes prime minister of Britain.
1939	In September, the Second World War begins.
1940	Winston Churchill becomes prime minister of Britain. Churchill names Beaverbrook minister of aircraft production and a member of the wartime cabinet.

1941	Aitken is named overall minister of production.
1942	Max resigns his office in a huff, is sent as an envoy to Washington (as lend-lease administrator), and pushes for a second front in the war.
1943	Aitken takes up agriculture.
1943–45	Beaverbrook is made Lord Privy Seal and an adviser to cabinet.
1945	Max's mistress, Jean Norton, dies. The Second World War ends. Clement Attlee becomes prime minister of Britain.
1947	Beaverbrook is named chancellor of the University of New Brunswick.
1949	Aitken resigns from the Conservative Party.
1951	Churchill becomes prime minister once again.
1963	Beaverbrook marries Lady Christofer Dunn, widow of Sir James Dunn.
1964, JUNE 9	Max Aitken dies

SOURCES

Aitken, Lord Beaverbrook, Max. *My Early Life* (Fredericton: Brunswick Press, 1965).

Bullock, Alan. *Hitler: A Study in Tyranny* (London: Penguin, 1990).

Churchill, Randolph. *Lord Derby, "King of Lancashire": The Official Life of Edward, Seventeenth Earl of Derby, 1865–1948* (London: Heinemann, 1959).

Howard, Peter. *Beaverbrook: A Study of Max the Unknown* (London: Hutchinson, 1964).

Jenkins, Roy. *Churchill: A Biography* (New York: Farrar, Strauss and Giroux, 2001).

Manchester, William. *The Last Lion: Winston Spencer Churchill: Alone, 1932–1940* (Boston and Toronto: Little, Brown, 1988).

Marchildon, Gregory P. *Profits and Politics: Beaverbrook and the Gilded Age of Canadian Finance.* (Toronto: University of Toronto Press, 1996).

Taylor, A.J.P. *Beaverbrook* (New York: Simon and Schuster, 1972).

COLLECT THEM ALL

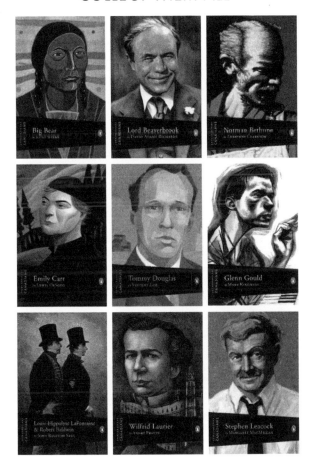

COLLECT THEM ALL